# Rugs from Rags

# Rugs from Rags

## John Hinchcliffe and Angela Jeffs

ORBIS PUBLISHING · London

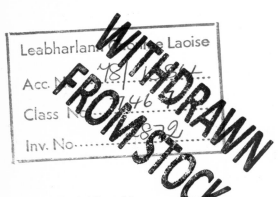
The Victoria and Albert Museum allocate
reference numbers to the rugs in their collection.
For your future reference the rugs from the Museum
which are shown in this book are numbered as
follows with the page number in parenthesis.
circ 354–1927 (page 20)
circ 529–1953 (page 21)
T11–1954 (page 40)
T149–1977 (page 91)

The publishers would like to acknowledge the help
of the following in permitting the use of
photographs shown on the pages listed.

The American Museum in Britain, Bath: 14, 15, 16, 17, 77
Beamish, North of England Open Air Museum: 18
Calderdale Museum's Service: 45
Mrs Clough, Partney, Lincs: 47
G. Dagli Orti/IGDA: 11
Mick Duff: 10
English Museum of Rural Life, University
of Reading, Maidie Hemeon Collection: 19, 33, 46
Institute of Geological Sciences: 11 left
Lervad (U.K.) Ltd: 37
Library of Congress, Washington D.C.: 35
Museum of Mankind, London: 80
Nordiska Museet, Stockholm: 12, 13, 75, 82, 83
Victoria and Albert Museum: 20, 21, 40, 90, 91

Studio photography by Peter Pugh-Cook
Illustrations by David Parr
Designed by Ingrid Mason

John Hinchcliffe would like to thank Nick Smith,
Eva Pettigrew, Jennifer Homer, Anna Watson and
Frances Hinchcliffe for helping to make the rugs
photographed for this book.

# Contents

# Foreword

Perhaps the greatest fascination for a working weaver lies in the vast number of types and qualities of materials available today. This feeling of excitement at the enormous potential of a craft is akin to that of a cabinet maker who chooses his woods with great care, knowing the grain, colour and quality that he will need and then, using a craftsman's experience, makes his own selection for the particular project.

In my own work, a feeling for colour and texture has always been crucial: I have experimented increasingly with different materials to achieve the surface qualities I specially look for in my rugs—concentrating particularly on cut cloth. My experiments have naturally led me to a study of the history of rag weaving and the many other traditional techniques employed in creating useful and beautiful things from old fabrics and clothes that would otherwise have been discarded.

It is my hope that this book, by showing examples of both traditional and modern work, and by demonstrating some of the many techniques available, will further stimulate the growing interest in this engrossing aspect of working with textiles.

John Hinchcliffe

# Introduction

It may be surprising to learn that the craft of making rugs and coverlets from rags—items of worn out clothing or simply remnants of natural and synthetic fabrics—is over 200 years old. And that the furnishings made in this way during the nineteenth century and in the early years of this century are now regarded as works of art, being seriously sought after and collected. Interesting too, that rags were regarded as being fairly valuable commodities; fabrics were not to be consumed in the modern sense and then discarded when their original function was outgrown or when fashion simply dictated newer fabrics and more interesting designs as has become the case in our own society.

After a period of affluence during which consumerism ran away with itself in the 1960s and the rubbish dumps of the world grew rich with valuable materials—wood, metals and fibres—we are now in a period of re-evaluation with a new practical appreciation of the importance of using our basic resources to best advantage, recycling as many materials as possible to extend their life and practical usefulness. The man and woman who ten years ago would have bought lengths of fabric to make new cushion covers are today more likely to root around in the scrap bag or utilize last year's fashion gimmick to make covers at no cost at all. Such is the economic and ecological climate of our time. As always, it is only when the materials we have taken for granted are in short supply that their true value and potential are realized and exploited to the full.

The English women who travelled to the New World on the Mayflower in 1620 created a completely new form of patchwork in order to make the most of the few scraps of fabric they were allowed to carry and display them to their best advantage. Each small piece was set in a window of coarse canvas, sacking or sailcloth to produce an interesting stained glass effect. Hence the name Cathedral patchwork. Many of our mothers and grandmothers will also remember having to 'make do and mend' when fabrics and clothing were in short supply during times of war or depression, stretching the life of materials by finding a variety of ingenious uses until the fibres literally disintegrated.

It was not unusual for a rag rug to be assembled by the family over the dark winter months for display in the front parlour after the annual spring cleaning. And each successive year it would be replaced, the old rug working its way over the years through all the rooms of the house in their order of importance.

But many of the surviving rugs that our ancestors made from necessity are today appreciated as primitive or even sophisticated works of art. And, as a result, there is not only a revival of interest in the techniques they employed, but also exciting new experiments to widen and extend the potential of the craft even further.

*Left and right: It is hard to believe that the beautiful woven rug on the left has been created from the waste product on the right—rags—that would otherwise have been thrown away but for the imagination and skill of John Hinchcliffe. This book will we hope encourage you to try rugmaking techniques and so inspire you to look upon the raw materials with interest*

When John Hinchcliffe studied weaving at the Royal College of Art in London, he introduced rags into his work as a result of a visit to Sweden, where he was fascinated and seduced by the intricate beauty of their rag textiles. As a result, his work is now regarded as being at the forefront of modern rag weaving and it is exhibited and sold all over the world. And though he finds it somewhat ironic that his rugs tend to end up as wall-hangings to be admired and protected as potential investments rather than being put to the practical use for which they were originally intended, his interest in all the techniques by which rugs can be made has increased. It is his genuine enthusiasm for the subject that is the reason for this book.

He lives in the quiet countryside of Sussex, drawing inspiration for his work not only from his immediate surroundings, but also from other more sophisticated and often unexpected sources. He is fascinated by the multi-coloured richness of mosaic, patchwork, textiles and painting; he enjoys studying the effect of light and shade on woodland and grass, and marvels at the intricate patternings in minerals and geological strata. The close relationship between all these stimuli and the highly complex results of his work with coloured and patterned pieces of fabric to produce pile and flat rugs are easy to appreciate. They are also an exciting starting point for anyone being introduced to the craft for the very first time.

*John Hinchcliffe experiments with various types of pile, seeing close similarities between the effects he tries to achieve and, on the one hand a field of corn with its random spiky texture, and on the other the softer and more subtle colouring of leaves with their ever changing pattern of light and shade. Likewise he is influenced by the multi-coloured diversity of nature—a bowl of pot pourri, or art—patchwork, mosaic or works of artists such as Matisse or Vuillard who were obsessed by the richness of textiles within room settings. And then unexpected oddities like the vase with its beautiful striations*

A variety of craft techniques can be used to recycle rags, not only into beautiful rugs, but into other furnishings too—cushions and hangings, for instance, and even articles of clothing and fashion accessories. The majority are inexpensive, requiring a minimum of tools, and most are quick and easy to learn and to apply, weaving apart. This book reveals the enormous range of possibilities and the creative potential of working with rags, giving detailed instructions for prodding or hooking pile rugs, plaiting or braiding flat rugs, knitting pile and flat surfaced rugs, and weaving rugs on various types of loom.

With the basic skills mastered, the most important thing to remember is that there are no rules.

The joy of the craft is its accidental nature. For anyone who values originality, there is the delightful satisfaction of knowing that whatever is created, it is unique. After all, no individual collection of rags, saved over the years can match another. Even if, by some extraordinary fluke of nature this should happen, the possibility that the rags should be accidentally assembled into identical rugs is too unlikely even to contemplate.

True creative satisfaction can be derived from building up pile, changing colour or extending the design of the rug as it develops. And if you do demand a greater control over the craft, dyeing enables the medium to be extended into a sophisticated art.

# The History of Rag Rugs

Although making rugs from rags has not been well-documented until recently, there are many examples to study and copy from both the old and new worlds. The Swedes particularly have made this traditional craft their own

The origins of using rags for thrift and economy is shrouded in history, few examples having survived from any earlier than the eighteenth century. But the roots do seem to be firmly entrenched in three main areas: northern Europe, northern England and colonial America. This would indicate that the origins were essentially European, the development of the use of rags in craft work being a direct result of the climate and the need to make the most of available materials. Most families of poor to average income from 1700 onwards lived in sparsely furnished homes built of wood or local stone, the floors being bare except on holidays, when they might be scattered with rush or sand brushed into designs and patterns.

Because the processes of making textiles from raw wool and flax were so complex, the resulting clothing, bedding and linens were valued highly and considered far too precious to be trampled underfoot. Carpets—stitched and pile—were available to only the wealthiest of families, and even straw mats and painted canvas floor coverings were financially out of reach of the major part of the population. All fabrics, before machines and mass-production techniques were introduced in the nineteenth century, were spun and woven by hand and were therefore expensive. Thus it was an economic necessity in many homes to make the most of the limited amounts of material available.

Most women, particularly in the countryside and poorer regions, were taught to spin and weave, and once clothing became outgrown or linens worn, it would have been natural to investigate ways of re-using them to domestic and economic advantage.

It is in Sweden that the earliest records of rag weaving exist, and it is a technique the Swedes have made very much their own. It is reasonable to assume that the emergence of rag weaving in America was the direct result of Swedish settlers introducing their native craft to the immigrant community.

The earliest existing example of rag weaving located to date is a Swedish counterpane with 1834 woven into the fabric itself. But it is known that the craft was practised a great deal earlier, for it is on record that in 1773, Lars Oloffson's wife Katarina of See left a piece of 'tatter weaving' in her will. And for more up-to-date evidence, a Swedish woman now living in England can recall her grandmother's house in Sweden where all the rugs and stair carpets had been made by *her* grandparents, dating them at the very latest 1750, and probably a lot earlier.

The technique of weaving with rags has changed little over the centuries since those early days. The fabric was cut into strips about an inch (2.5cm) wide and woven into a linen or cotton weft, the ends being joined as the work progressed. The basic weaves used were tabby, twill and simple patterning to introduce motifs. Because of the limited width of the looms used, the resulting narrow strips of cloth were ideal for floors, corridors and stairs or as decoration and cover for the tops of chests and cupboards. It was a fairly obvious move to stitch the strips together to form larger pieces, so the technique proved ideal for coverlets and blankets. There is even evidence of similar larger pieces known as 'sea rugs' being used by sailors as capes. And by about 1920, huge rugs were being assembled to resemble carpets.

*Left: No Swedish home was ever conisdered satisfactorily furnished without at least one length of rag weaving in each room. Long pieces were laid on floors and in corridors, while smaller strips were used more decoratively on table tops and linen chests*

*These three rugs show the development in the intricacy of design during the nineteenth century. The primitive rug above is dated about 1825; the floral rug on the left was worked on canvas in about 1850; in the later rug on the right there is still a floral motif but it is now placed within a strong yet intricate geometric grid, a design element that is now established*

Weaving, and more particularly rag weaving, is now regarded as Sweden's major traditional craft, and not only are old textiles carefully preserved, but modern experiments are encouraged at every level, whether in the home, studio or factory. Just as Marta Helena Reenstierna recorded in her local journal in 1916 that 'the wife of Boberg has woven simple mats of rags, hair spun into yarn, horsehair and other collected rubbish', weavers are now using their ingenuity to equally practical but presumably more aesthetic ends, incorporating all manner of natural and synthetic materials into their work. Swedish rugs and woven textiles are now a major export, not only prized for their beauty and brave dramatic use of colour, but their practical durability too.

Just as bed rugs and coverlets were highly valued in Swedish homes, so they played an important role in the use of rags in American crafts. English needlework skills and the Swedish tradition of rag weaving merged to effect in the New World. Until about 1820 the word 'rugg' referred to a coarsely woven woollen cloth or bedcover, and most 'ruggs' made during the eighteenth and early nineteenth centuries were used on the bed or on other pieces of furniture, never on the floor. This was because the bed was the most important piece of furniture in the pioneer home, so its decoration was of prime importance. Indeed it became the focal point of all the woman's technical and creative skills.

# History

Various techniques were employed, a bedcover being the basic requirement of every girl's bottom drawer in preparation for marriage and setting up her own home. So, whether quilted, of pieced patchwork or appliquéd, stitched or sewn, it was an opportunity for creative endeavour, the designs, motifs and pictorial contents being generally drawn from the creator's surroundings and the way of life of the period. Very few of these 'ruggs' survive today—fewer than 50 is the generally accepted estimate. And many of these incorporate rags in some way or another, often combined with one or more of the techniques previously described.

The beginning of the nineteenth century saw mills springing up all over New England, and

*Below: The American Civil War occurred at a time when rag rug making was at its height of popularity, and its theme spawned a whole crop of rugs declaring a political bias. This fairly primitive rug has a light on dark outer border, and then the floral garland is repeated in reverse on the lighter central part of the rug. The Union flag takes pride of place in the centre with the word added for good measure*

though cheaper cottons and woollens became more readily available the thrift conscious—and this was usually due to necessity rather than any artistic drive—still utilized odd scraps and old clothing to make new bedcovers. Then, around 1830, the mills began producing carpeting and the vogue for floor coverings spread rapidly. Those unable to afford manufactured carpets began to look to their scrap bags for ways to create rugs.

It was during this period that shirred and braided rugs came into existence. Shirring—an appliqué technique—developed because cloth strips were so much thicker than yarn that they could not be worked through a woven base with a needle. A 'chenille' method was employed, strips being prepared with a row of running stitches along the centre of each length and then gathered up to resemble furry caterpillars. These were then stitched onto a base of cotton, linen or rough sacking. A second method involved cutting the fabric into bias strips and then sewing the lengthwise centre fold of each one to a base so that the raw edges were uppermost. Both these techniques were popular between 1820 and 1860, then declined with the introduction of hooking scraps into a burlap foundation. Both shirring and hooking used rags, but the latter technique proved to be more durable and easier to work, allowing greater flexibility in handling the rug and creating a design.

Similar and even more ingenious methods of sewing scraps proved popular in Scotland and the north of England from the late nineteenth century well into the twentieth century. The idea of pulling strips of cloth through a loosely woven base is akin to tambour work, an embroidery technique that originated in the Orient, but was used extensively by many European and American women between 1780 and 1860. Other sources suggest that sailors may have influenced their wives to put the marlin spike—a tool used in ropework—to more domestic use. Indeed, many of the tools that survive today are similar in shape to the marlin and are used in much the same way.

As linen was too close a weave to hook through with ease, it was not until jute became a regular import into America around 1850 that the technique really came into its own. The open loose weave of burlap and the strength of jute proved an ideal combination. As a result, hooked rugs have been regarded by many as 'America's one indigenous folk art'; the long held belief that it originated in England has been challenged by several leading authorities on the subject. And their point does seem to be verified by the lack of existing old rugs or references to the craft in old records and literature. Let the English claimants score a point, however, in noting that Mrs Gaskell, in chapter eight of her novel *Cranford* published in 1851, described Carl (the dog) as lying on 'the twisted marled rug'.

*Top: Animals were always a popular subject in rug making and one of the most popular of the commercial designs was a lion. As many people preferred to create their own designs, they simply copied the basic theme and then improvised. This delightful North American rug is known as 'Lion and Beavers', thus mixing mythology with an animal rather closer to home*

*Above: Horses too featured in many rag rugs. This creature, dramatically dappled, prances across the rug and is captured mid-gallop. It was made in the mid-nineteenth century*

# History

The English, with their usual individuality, have compiled a variety of homespun methods for making mats and rugs, all deriving from the ancient technique of 'thrumming', a means of using up short pieces of waste yarn or thread. Depending on the area of the country or the particular county in which the craft developed, it became known as 'podging', 'pegging', 'prodding', 'brodding', 'probbing' and 'poking'. The resulting rugs had their own names too, 'cleekies' and 'druggetts', for example. A series of letters collected from various parts of the country in response to an appeal for old rugs or references to them resulted in some fascinating information about the ingenious ways the rugs were put together.

A woman in Suffolk still makes rag rugs on her sewing machine (but sadly doesn't explain quite how!), whereas a woman in Staffordshire recalls that apart from a needle and thread she used only a very large safety pin. Another northerner remembers that in 1934 she lodged in a house near Castleford, the landlady of which had a fine rug she had pegged with a tool like a giant nail and as thick as the woman's little finger. She had cut the pieces of felt so that each was slightly curved and pointed at both ends, claiming that this prevented too much dust being trapped in the pile. The scraps of felt had come from the mills in Dewsbury, Batley and Morley, where felt and shoddy—cheap cloth made from re-used rags—were made.

*Right: A northern woman now living near Oxford in England prodded this rug in a mixture of cotton and woollen fabrics some thirty years ago and it is still giving good wear. She overlapped dinner plates for the main part of the design and then worked the rest by improvisation*

*Below: These two women from the north of England are working a prodded rug on a make-shift frame which uses a fence and trestle for support*

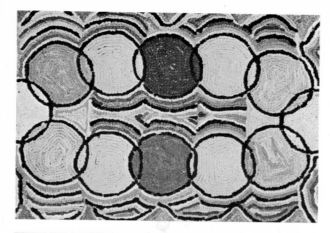

Below: The designer wanted a rug to fit specifically into a doorway and around a fireplace. She drew the outline on the base fabric and prodded it in the usual way, then cut around the piece made to shape and backed it for hard wear. The simple brickwork pattern is in a mixture of cotton, woollen and synthetic rags

Left: At the Beamish Museum in the north of England, interior settings of miners' cottages reflect the working and domestic way of life in the late nineteenth and early twentieth century. In one, a frame supporting a partly worked hooked rug is on the table while finished rugs lie before the fire and over the floor

Right: The 'hooky' rug is exclusive to the north of England and instantly recognizable by its deep cut pile and shaggy appearance. Few are still in existence due to the habit of a rug being passed from room to room each year until completely worn out.

A man from Rugby remembered his mother making rag rugs in the summer to put on the beds in the winter. 'We were', he recalled nostalgically, 'ever so warm!' Another woman had seen a complete stair carpet made by the hooking method in Northumberland. And a Tynesider defined a 'hooky' rug as being one worked using long strips of cloth, while a 'clippie' had small pieces worked into the wrong side of the base fabric. Obviously this shows a real diversity of methods, none with any greater merit than another. All of them resulted in practical rugs—and that was always the prime consideration in British rag rugs.

The making of rag rugs has always been something of a home industry since its earliest beginnings. There are records of Swedish craftsmen and women trading locally in woven pieces, just as there are in America. Many thousands of yards of rag carpeting were woven in Canada from about 1880 onwards. As fabrics became more readily available, people would prepare their own rags and then take them to the local weaver.

One woman, visited in 1947, had two looms, both two shaft. She had been taught to weave by her mother, an early Irish immigrant, and since the only craft product in demand locally was rag carpeting, she had woven them to order for over 70 years. Persuaded to bring out her box of precious samples, it quickly became apparent that more interesting effects could be achieved with a rag carpet than any average weaver could ever dream possible.

Hooked and prodded rugs also proved a valuable source of income, both in North America and the north of England. Many communities were at the mercy of an extreme climate and unreliable local industries. In coastal regions, people were used to spending snowbound winters repairing nets, making tools, and involving themselves in crafts during the dark evenings. It is not surprising that in many places simple skills soon achieved a level of artistry and quality that cannot have been appreciated at the time: they were certainly not regarded as being worth a mention in magazines and periodicals, even those concerned with needlecraft and associated subjects.

Hooked rugs were regarded everywhere as being very much a 'country' or 'working class' craft, the results being far too inferior for use and display in smart American or Victorian households. And they had found no place at all in England until the very end of the nineteenth century, which was quite a time after they had reached the peak of their popularity in North America. Many English rugs were influenced by the commercial stencilled designs printed on burlap that American mail-order companies like Sears, Roebuck and Montgomery Ward offered in their catalogues in the 1890s, many of which reached the British Isles. Thus true creativity was stemmed at the very beginning, and as a result, English rugs never reached the level of artistic integrity found in many of the American 'primitive' rugs.

Although some people may feel that this is a matter for concern, it should be remembered that the history of the English rag rug is equally rich, but in a rather different way. Skilled technicians and artists no longer regard homecrafts as unsophisticated and unworthy of serious consideration; many of them are increasingly happy to use home-grown techniques to display their more recognized talents. It is this area that is proving the most interesting in the twentieth century.

*Right: A boldly patterned rag rug made in 1953 and reflecting the growing interest in 'modern' design after the visual deprivations of the two world wars. It is English and was designed and worked by John and Lucie Aldridge*

*Below: A silk and cotton woven rug from Sweden dated 1930. The colouring is delightfully subtle, the patterning equally so*

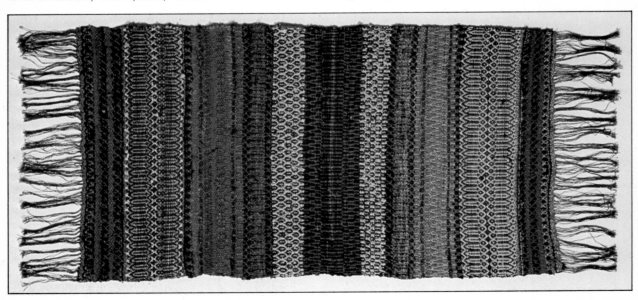

# Preparing Rags

Before beginning your rag rug, it is necessary to collect and sort your rags according to weight, texture and colour and then make your selection. John Hinchcliffe also gives guidance on dyeing techniques and colour co-ordination ideas for you

The term rags is slightly misleading. The dictionary defines rags as being 'torn or frayed pieces of woven material'. To most people this means waste or scrap. But in the context of this book, rags mean any piece of fabric, usually remnants of clothing or furnishing fabric that are either natural or synthetic in origin, plain or printed, woven, knitted or bonded.

Although the selection of rags is not important in itself because the rugs made from them are more the result of a haphazard use of materials, your choice should be determined by two factors. Some of the techniques in this book require large pieces of rag, others quite small ones. And if you intend dyeing any fabrics, in which case good colour and resistance to fading is essential, you will need to match a fabric to the most suitable dye. If you do not intend to use dyes, you can be less selective and mix types of fabric with impunity.

Anyone who sews will probably have accumulated remnants and scraps already. Alternatively, old clothing is the most rewarding source. Anything that is stained should be discarded, however, especially if it is to be dyed. The stain, being an unknown quantity, may resist the dye or turn the cloth an unexpected colour.

Remove all buttons, zips and trimmings from clothing, and tear or cut away all seams, hems, pockets, belts and sleeves, so that you are left with flat pieces of rag. Many of the items you have removed can be re-used at a later date. Any badly worn parts should be cut away and discarded. Rags should be washed to remove the dirt and any finish that has been used on the cloth and might resist a dye later on. Test a small corner first to make sure the existing colour does not run. This would not prove disastrous if a single piece were washed on its own, but certainly would if it is washed with other materials. To have rags tainted with a colour that is not fast could ruin the end result since you will almost certainly want to wash your rug at some time or another. Once washed and dried, try to sort your fabrics into categories: cottons, woollens, silks and synthetics. This process requires a knowledge of the structure and content of fibres. With experience, however, you should soon be able to recognize fabrics by their appearance and texture and to sort them with confidence and expertise.

John Hinchcliffe tends to use mainly natural fibres in his rugs: cotton, which is a vegetable fibre, and wool, which is an animal fibre. He finds them more responsive to dyes and keeping to one or two types cuts the cost of dyeing experimentally. He buys his rags from a rag merchant who collects and sells mainly to the paper and textile industry. He is able to pick and choose, keeping a special eye open for old fabrics with interesting prints, texture and weave. He finds this recycling aspect of his work both rewarding and stimulating, and takes as much pleasure in discovering unusual pieces of rag within the pile as did entire families in former years, who would spend long winter evenings identifying pieces from the family wardrobe in their hooked and prodded rugs.

As you will probably collect your rags in more domestic circumstances, beg, borrow and buy from friends, and in rummage and jumble sales. If you live in a large city, find out where the 'rag trade' or fashion industry makes up clothing and try to get hold of their off-cuts and trimmings.

Rag weaving grew out of a need to be sparing with textiles, and with the high cost of all raw materials today, there is increasing interest in ways to use and re-use the whole range of fibres. We have all become so used to wearing out and then throwing away, that it is sobering to consider the lengths women went to in the past to waste nothing. In Sweden, for instance, they unravelled woollen textiles and pounded them in a wooden churn of hot water (known as a rag churn) so that the threads and individual fibres loosened and the wool returned to shoddy. This was dried, carded, spun into yarn and finally rewoven into cloth.

Your handling of fabrics will give you experience in learning to distinguish between one fabric and another by weight as well as appearance and feel. It is best to work with materials of similar weight to begin with, as it takes time to learn to mix them so as to achieve an overall balanced effect. You will soon be able to gauge the width of a piece of lightweight fabric that will balance a thinner strip in tweed, however, and this will add even greater interest to your rugs.

## Textural Qualities

According to its dictionary definition, the word texture is derived from the Latin *textura*, meaning 'web' or 'woven'. In more recent times, however, it has taken on a more general meaning, referring not only to the surface of textiles, but to all other objects too. We use texture in referring to the smooth skin of an apple or the close-cropped stubble left in a field after harvesting. It has entered our language as something we respond to with our senses, through sight, touch and even sound.

Texture is basic to John Hinchcliffe's work. He is not concerned with creating a woven base, but inserting into this web dyed and undyed rags

*Above: Whatever your source of fabrics, be fairly selective, choose them for their fibre content, range of pattern and colouring, their weight and texture. All these rags, which John Hinchcliffe is considering for a particular rug, are in pure cotton*

to create a deep and richly textured pile. As a result, his rugs can be viewed to equal effect from a distance for an overall appreciation of the design as a whole, or from close at hand, where a more detailed inspection reveals a secret world of patterns and prints within the pile itself. So an appreciation of texture is as important as being sensitive and familiar with colour and line.

Awareness of textures can be increased simply by a deliberate concentration of the senses, and this will add a new dimension to rug making. After all, it is as important for you to be able to distinguish one fabric from another and one surface from another as it is for a gardener to be able to differentiate between a clay and sandy soil, by sight and touch. Tactile differences will quickly become familiar, this recognition making you more confident and your work more rewarding.

As a simple exercise, take a group of fabrics at random, close your eyes and stroke them with the tips of your fingers. A nap or pile that seems to run more naturally in one direction than the other may be a velvet or suede-type fabric, such as chenille or velour. A shiny smooth surface may be a satin or glazed cotton; something light that almost squeaks when stroked is probably a pure silk or rayon. A rough and open weave that grazes the skin if stroked too firmly could be a hessian or coarse sacking.

By using your eyes you can appreciate the effect of light and shade on each type of textile. Satin will shimmer, appearing to be almost white when looked at from a certain angle. A loose wool appears warm and comforting; other fabrics give the impression of being cold before they are touched, and the action of touching simply confirms or contradicts the initial impression. All these factors are elements of texture, and bring the full range of our senses into play.

The range of techniques used in rag rug making can result in a variety of textures too. A plaited or braided rug in wool will look and feel very different to one made in cotton or silk. And the mixing of one fabric with another can result in rugs with very interesting textures.

John Hinchcliffe uses cotton rags in his rug making and is fascinated by the depth and feel of the pile he creates. Sometimes he inserts the rags close to each other for a firm upright pile; at other times he prefers a looser, less resistant pile and so the rags are spaced further apart. The surface is made additionally interesting by the fraying of the cut edges of the rags, the light playing subtle tricks on the resulting uneven surface. Prodding or plaiting rugs can result in very different types of texture, depending on the tension applied in the technique or whether the cut edges of the rags are allowed to remain on the surface or are tucked away inside the loops of braids. And again, each rug will differ according to the fabrics used. You may already have a preference for a particular textural effect. John Hinchcliffe prefers cotton rags, but you may enjoy the warmer feel of wool.

## Colour Selection

The impact of John Hinchcliffe's rugs is immediate. Not only are they attractive because of their rich textural qualities and the multitude of prints and patterns within the pile, but also because of the carefully predetermined relationship of colours in the overall design. The fact that his rugs stimulate the eye—sometimes with subtlety, often boldly, always with confidence—is the result of careful planning, though at the same time allowing for an infinite variety of colourful but controlled accidents within the pile itself.

He achieves these effects by means of careful dyeing. Obviously his approach varies according to each individual project. He may be asked by a private individual or interior designer to execute a rug in an existing colour scheme to complement and enhance a particular room or range of furnishings. Or he may be invited to design a rug or series of rugs for exhibition purposes, allowing him far greater flexibility.

John Hinchcliffe regards colour as one of three major factors to be considered when planning and designing a rug. First, the materials must be decided upon. Then the technique is selected, in his case it is weaving, though there are others, of course including knitting, prodding, plaiting or crochet. Alternatively, you could experiment to find an entirely new method. Finally, he considers the colours to be integrated into his design, and decides whether to use undyed rags, dyed rags, or the two together.

It is probably best not to dwell too seriously upon your choice of colours to begin with, but simply to take heart from the fact that most creators of old rugs knew nothing of colour as a science. They simply drew their inspiration from the materials to hand and from their experience of community or family life and nature. With great naivety, they achieved remarkable results by the simplest and most direct means. If a red was required, it hardly seemed a matter of great concern that an exact shade was not available. And if one shade of a colour ran out, another shade or one in harmony or even complete contrast could be introduced. Yet in spite of, or perhaps because

of, this haphazard approach, rugs of great inherent charm were produced.

Such accidental effects have much in common with nature itself. Look at a dappled landscape changing under a cloudy sky or a mass of blooms in a garden. Ask a child what colour a tree is and he or she will answer brown and green. Look at the leaves in detail, however, and an infinite range of subtle shades, tints and hues will reveal themselves to you.

For those who prefer a more scientific approach to colour, it is useful to have a basic appreciation of a few facts. White light is made up of the visible spectrum containing the full range of colours in all their hues. The addition of black results in shade, and white, tint. The mixing of one colour with another can result in an entirely new colour—adding yellow to blue results in a green, for instance. This is something you will need to understand in more detail when dyeing fabrics.

John Hinchcliffe studied initially as an artist and knows from experience the optical effect of placing one colour against another. He plans his rugs in the same way that an artist visualizes and conceptualizes a painting. The range of colour combinations is infinite, and it can be exciting and rewarding to explore.

Your reasons for assembling a group or range of colours in relation to one another within a design may be quite spontaneous, with little regard for what looks right or wrong. You can allow your

*Below: John Hinchcliffe plans colourways for a rug by creating a sampler—or samplers—of pre-dyed rag. This enables him to not only see the results of new recipes and trials, but to place and arrange colours in relation to one another in an experimental situation. The piece illustrated is dyed in a range of colours of approximately the same tonal value*

*Right: The colours in this detail from one of his rag rugs positively glows, jewel-like. The colours, graded from light to dark in each individual strip, form a regular design once the pieces are sewn together*

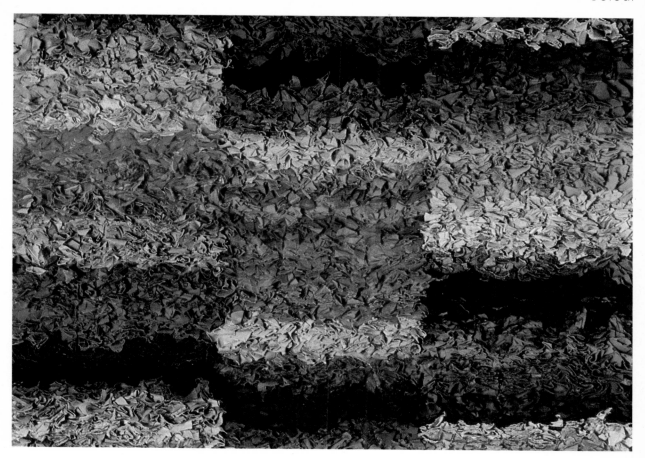

approach to be passionate in its attack and flair, placing colours together to excite and flaunt convention, in total defiance of any rules. Your choice can be entirely personal, choosing colours simply because you prefer one colour or a range of colours to another. Whatever you do, however, it is always useful to keep a record of your experiments in colour, both for reference and as a stimulus for later work.

For successful colour combinations, it is often advisable to back purely emotional responses with some sound common sense tempered by scientific fact and proven evidence. When devising colour schemes and themes, many artists, designers and craftsmen refer to a simple diagrammatic colour system based on the spectrum of colours which occurs naturally in daylight. The system usually employed is the colour circle.

In a simplified version of this system, colours are divided into twelve distinct hues, each in its allotted position in the natural spectrum. First of all there are the primary colours from which all other colours are derived: red, blue and yellow. Then there are the secondary colours—orange, green and violet, which are mixtures of the primary hues. Finally, the circle is completed by the addition of the colours that lie between the primaries and secondaries, such as reddish-orange or yellowish-orange, yellowish-green or bluish-green, and so on. Using such a colour circle, it is relatively easy to devise effective colour

schemes. For example, you can achieve simple harmonies by choosing a range of colours built around a basic colour, such as red, reddish-violet and reddish-orange. Alternatively, you can place colours which appear opposite one another in the circle for the greatest possible colour contrasts. These can be quite spectacular in effect.

More subtle effects can be achieved by relating the deeper, richer tones of the tertiary colours (mixtures or pairs of secondary colours). The resulting colours range through russets, citrons and olive greens.

Fascinating and unexpected harmonies and discords can result when the hues of the colour circle are not used in their pure state. There are, of course, enormous and complex ramifications to colour theory, but the simple ideas given here will help you create compositions. It is enough to remember that contrasting colours will provide the maximum vibrancy, while harmony will result from using colours that are closely related. Colour is the most effective means of establishing a 'mood' for your work with rags.

If you read as much as you can on the subject of colour and do simple exercises to understand the tricks that colour can play on the eye, you will increase your colour awareness. You will be able to move your fabrics around in contrasting and harmonious relationships to one another to explore their full potential. It is time well spent, and can improve your sensitivity to colour.

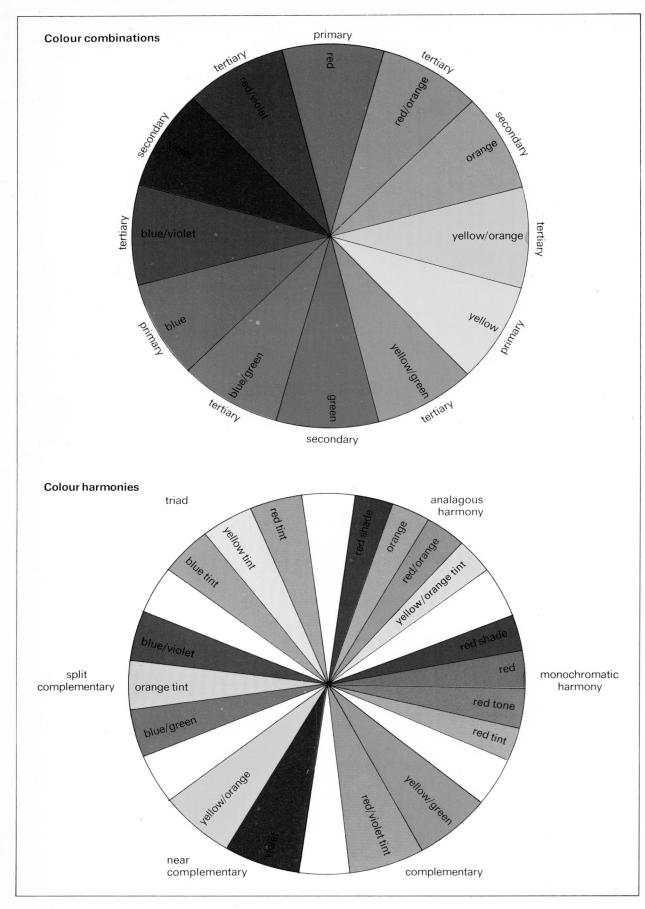

**Colour combinations**

primary — red
tertiary — red/violet
secondary — violet
tertiary — blue/violet
primary — blue
tertiary — blue/green
secondary — green
tertiary — yellow/green
primary — yellow
tertiary — yellow/orange
secondary — orange
tertiary — red/orange

**Colour harmonies**

triad
analagous harmony
red tint
yellow tint
blue tint
red shade
orange
red/orange
yellow/orange tint
blue/violet
orange tint
red shade
red
split complementary
blue/green
red tone
red tint
yellow/orange
violet
red/violet tint
yellow/green
near complementary
complementary
monochromatic harmony

## A Guide to Dyeing

The creation of textiles in the past involved numerous processes, each one an individual craft in its own right. First the raw materials were collected, then the fibres combed and carded, spun into yarn or thread, dyed to decorative effect and finally woven into cloth.

All these processes were and still are time-consuming if done by hand, but they can all be rewarding in their own ways. None, however, can be more stimulating than dyeing—the art of changing colour of a fabric or yarn by means of artificially introduced pigments. If you are following John Hinchcliffe's lead and intending to hand dye the rags prior to using them, it is essential to grasp the nature of individual dyes and understand their effect on different fabrics and fibres. If it is of no particular importance to you that the immersion of a red printed fabric in a yellow dye results in orange cloth, then no matter: the unexpected results of dyeing will be mysterious and delightful, and the finished rug equally so. John Hinchcliffe, however, though he works partly by instinct, initially designs and plans his rugs with considerable precision. Experience and practical know-how enables him to control his dyes with skill and so achieve the effects required for a particular design.

Dyes tend to have a natural affinity for a certain type of fibre, and if this affinity is not present, the fibre will reject the dye and colouring will not take place. Therefore, if you require a certain colour or fabric in a particular rug, you must make sure to use the correct dye.

There are basically two types of dye: chemical and natural. Likewise, there are two types of fibre. Natural fibres can be divided into animal and vegetable, the former including wool, silk and numerous hair fibres such as goat and camel. These are often known as protein fibres being protein based. Vegetable fibres include cotton, linen, jute and sisal, and are sometimes classed as cellulosic fibres being cellulose based. The man-made fibre viscose rayon is also cellulose based being made from wood pulp. The other type of fibre, the purely synthetic fibres, can be grouped

*Left: Colour wheels are always useful, not only for a scientific appreciation and understanding of how colours mix to produce secondary and tertiary colours, but how they can be used to harmonious effect. John Hinchcliffe uses a particular wheel that not only gives the colours in all their harmonies, but all their gradations from light to shade, called tones, as well. Collect as many charts as you can—those supplied by paint companies are often excellent—and use them to guide you to satisfactory colourways in your rugs*

as polyamide fibres such as nylon; polyester fibres such as terylene or dacron; and acrylics such as acrilan or orlon.

The simplest method for identifying fabrics is by burning them. Fibres of an animal or protein will not burn easily, and a black bead forms, giving off the very characteristic smell of burning feathers. Fibres of a vegetable or cellulose origin burn readily and continue to burn when withdrawn from the flame. They smell more like paper being burnt.

Obviously, this test is merely an indication, a guide, because fabrics are often mixes, for instance the warp may be cotton while the weft is wool. Further research may well be necessary to make quite sure that a fibre is what it seems, otherwise a dye might not take.

Various types of dye are available. They range from ordinary household hot and cold water dyes that are easy to use but unreliable in colour and fastness, to expensive brands that have excellent colour ranges and a reliability that make them popular with artists and craftsmen who demand a high standard in their materials.

Using dyes is very much a matter of following the manufacturer's instructions. Their dyes are all the result of careful laboratory testing, so they do know what they are talking about when they recommend their dye for a certain fabric or suggest certain methods of dyeing.

The colour you can dye a rag is dependant on the original colour of the rag. Here are a list of suggestions as to which colour dye you should buy and match with your rags:
White will turn the colour of the dye being used; yellows will dye to green, orange, red, navy blue, brown and maroon; reds will dye maroon, deep brown, navy blue, purples and crimson; beiges will dye red, brown, dark brown, maroon, dark green and navy blue; brown can only dye a darker shade of brown; pale blues dye bright navy blue, brown and dark brown and dark green; bright blues can only be dyed a dark navy blue; pale greens dye emerald green, dark green, deep brown and navy blue; dark greens dye only darker greens; and any colour will dye black.

John Hinchcliffe also works with natural dyes, but he finds the work involved in extracting large quantities of pigment time-consuming and un-economic. In creative terms, however, there is no doubt that natural dyes can be well worth the effort. The whole process becomes more per-sonally satisfying and the resulting shades of dye can be beautifully subtle.

One of John Hinchcliffe's favourite natural dyes is indigo, a blue obtainable from certain plants. Indigo, along with madder and cochineal, is one of the oldest dyeing agents known to man and it is still relatively cheap to buy. Until about 1850, the development of dyeing was limited both by the local availability of materials and the restricted technical means of using them effec-tively. Around that date, William Henry Perkin discovered mauve, a by-product of coal tar, and this was put to use as the first aniline dye. As a result, the latter part of the nineteenth century saw a revolution in dyeing. The new dyes of chemical or synthetic composition were easier to use and more dependable, so natural dyes regressed to being simply a hobby. The recent resurgence of interest in country crafts is seeing a return to natural dyes, however, and more and more people are researching into folklore to learn how to extract them.

If you decide to explore the full range of natural dyes, you will have to collect flowers, leaves and berries, barks and lichens, fruit and vegetables. By simmering them for varying lengths of time you can extract their dye and colour. Some plants can be used for direct dyeing, others will require the assistance of a mordant to fix the dye in the fabric. The word mordant is derived from the French verb *mordre*—'to bite'. The best known mordants are alum, iron and tin, though there are many others, and most are available from good pharmacies.

Whether using chemical or natural dyes, it is a good idea to keep a record of your experiments, mounting the results in a book with relevant notes where appropriate. Observe some general rules when beginning to dye your rags. Start by experimenting with household dyes and then progress to the others. Always use plenty of dye liquor in relation to the fabric being dyed. If you try to stuff too much fabric into too small a vessel, the fabric will be patchy. Use a ratio of 30 parts water to one part fabric. This is best measured by weight, using ounces and fluid ounces or, on the metric system, grammes and litres. Weigh the material and multiply by 30 to compute the amount of water necessary. Keep the fabric moving and dye slowly. Do not rush.

You should use soft water wherever possible, adding a softening agent, if the water is too hard. Always wash fabric prior to dyeing any finishes or chemicals could resist new colour, and never dye it dry. Bring a dye to boiling point slowly and then leave the fabric immersed for an average of 20 minutes, but always experiment for the correct strength.

The strength or depth of shade is controlled by the weight of the dyestuff in proportion to the fabric, not by the amount of water in the dyebath. Never add dye powder to the dyebath. Simply mix the dye to a paste with cold water and then add cold water gradually. This is important to remember.

The strength of a dye is usually referred to as a percentage. If, for instance, you use three grammes of dyestuff to dye fabric weighing 100g, this is a percentage of three in 100 for a three per cent shade. You can thus work out in advance how much dye is required for a particular weight of fabric as follows:

$$\frac{\text{weight of fabric}}{100} \times \text{percentage} = \text{weight of dye}$$

As an example, imagine that you want to dye an amount of fabric weighing 238g for a five per cent shade, and work it out as follows:

$$\frac{238 \times 5}{100} = \frac{238}{20} = 11 \cdot 9g \text{ of the dyestuff}$$

Obviously to make such decisions you will need to be able to recognize and distinguish a three per cent shade from one that is only two per cent, so work methodically and keep a pattern book of all the colours and their effect on different fabrics. You can then increase or decrease the percentage of dye you use when a lighter or darker shade is called for in a particular project.

Remember also, before dyeing any fabric, gather together a stainless steel bucket, a glass or wooden stick for constant stirring, a liquid measure, spoons and a glass jar for mixing the dye.

*Below right: Dyeing certainly allows you more control for creating pre-planned rugs in particular colourways. The rags will lose their initial 'sparkle' but gain a certain element of mystery. From a distance the eye sees the specific colour as intended, but within this can be seen the original patterning and colouring*

*Below: Using undyed rags results in a very different effect. Even from a distance there is a spontaneity, a continual stimulation of the senses*

| Type of dye | Nature and solubility | Fibres |
|---|---|---|
| Natural dyes | There are certain dyeplants which have subtle colours but are rather unpredictable and other vegetable and animal dyes such as indigo, which is recommended for wool and cotton, and fustic, cochineal, madder and cutch logwood. Hot or cold dyebath. | Most dye wool with a mordant. |
| Direct dyes | Versatile, easy to use, cheap. Hot dyebath. | Affinity for cellulosic fibres, though will dye silk and wool. |
| Vat dyes | Very fast, resistant to light and washing. Cold dyebath, though some are insoluble. | Cellulosic fibres only, e.g. cotton and linen. |
| Mordant dyes | Their action depends on a mordant that combines with the dye to create colour. | Cotton or viscose. |
| Basic dyes | Cheap, easy to use. Vivid colours. They do have a poor resistance to light and washing. | Affinity with wool and silk. Can be used with a mordant for cotton. |
| Acid dyes (acetic acid) | Easy to use. Hot dyebath. | Wool and silk. |
| Reactive dyes (procion) | These react chemically with the fibres. They are very fast and easy to use. A hot or cold dyebath. | Best on cotton. |
| Dispense dyes | Easy to use. | Synthetics such as Cellulose Triacetate, Nylon, Terylene |
| Assorted household dyes | Relatively expensive. They are not recommended if you are intending to dye seriously and in quantity. | Effective on all types of fibres in some way. Rather unpredictable. |

## Preparing Materials

First you must decide on your working area. You will probably have to operate in more limited circumstances than the professional who usually has either a workroom or a studio in which to store his materials and equipment. Some of the techniques outlined in later projects require few tools and little room in which to use them successfully; others may threaten to take over your home. You can work a small prodded, hooked or knitted rug on your lap. In weaving there should be a natural progression from experimenting on a small frame to weaving small pieces on a table loom, finally advancing to more complex work on a full-size floor loom. Such looms are, of course, very expensive, and unless you are prepared to weave full-time, it would be wiser to use the facilities of a school, college or a specialist weaving studio. Of the latter there are an increasing number offering full- and part-time courses with excellent facilities.

Dyeing can be a fairly messy business, especially if you are working with large quantities of rags or yarn. Some dyes involve using heat, so a saucepan, bucket or larger vessel will be required. If the weather is good, it might be feasible to work outside though this would involve building a fire and constructing a support for the dye bath. Cold water dyes are obviously the easiest to use, so begin with these.

Use rubber gloves when dyeing, and cover yourself with an apron and the surrounding areas with newspapers. Dyes will stain other things apart from fabric, so take care. Whether dyeing cotton rags or wool yarn or rags, stir constantly to make sure the dye acts evenly. When judging the colour intensity, remember that the rags will dry to a lighter shade than they appear to have taken when wet.

Rinse the rags very thoroughly to get rid of excess dye until the water is quite clear. Otherwise the dyed fabrics could bleed later on and spoil the other rags in the finished article.

Dry natural fibres in a cool, shady place rather than in direct sunlight. You can then sort them into groups of colour for working and to aid selection, using boxes, drawers, baskets or simply piling them on the floor. You are now ready to begin your rug making.

To understand the nature and structure of textiles by practical experiment, take a piece of cotton cloth in your hands and pull across the width of the fabric so that it is taut. Fibres run the length (the warp threads) and width (the weft threads) of any piece of woven cloth. Therefore, if you feel a tension and the fabric runs smoothly from one side to another, you are working and pulling with the fibres, that is, with the grain. If the fabric stretches and puckers, you are probably pulling diagonally across the fibres, that is to say you are pulling on the bias or cross.

*Left: Having washed, dried and sorted your rags, organize them by colour or fibre content (or both) for ease of selection. Baskets or boxes will keep them together tidily, allowing instant access and will constantly be on view to stimulate ideas for new colourways and projects*

*Right: The next step is to cut the rags into strips. John Hinchcliffe is cutting his fabric on the bias—that is diagonally across the warp and weft rather than following them on the straight*

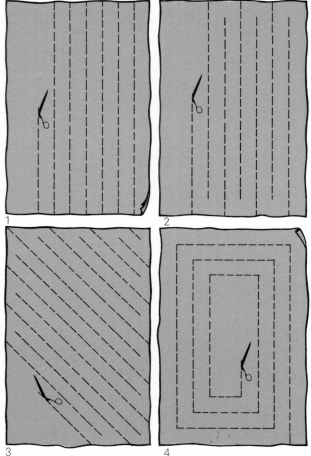

*Above: Here are four ways in which to cut a piece of fabric.*
*1 Cut lengthways strips parallel to the selvedge, called on the straight*
*2 Cut lengthways but as a long continuous strip. There will be a two cornered twist at each end where the fabric is not cut through completely. This will add texture to your rug*
*3 Cut diagonally from one corner to another, called on the bias*
*4 Alternatively, try cutting in a square working into the centre, or work in a spiral. Each method will add its own interest*

To cut cloth for rug making, each technique dictates a different approach. You will need to cut along the straight of the grain for individual strips, on the bias or cross for greater flexibility, in spirals for interesting textural effects, and in continuous lengths if you want to speed the work as much as possible. Experiment first in each case to determine the best method of cutting for each technique, using a pair of really sharp scissors. Electric scissors are particularly speedy and used by many modern rug makers. The width of the strips will depend very much on the type of fabric you are using and which technique is employed. In general you can cut strips between 7·5cm (3in) and 2·5cm (1in) wide. Usually, if the fabric is heavy, the strip will be narrow, and the lighter the material the wider you can cut it. Some fabrics will fray more easily than others. If you do not like the texture fraying produces, use fabrics which fray as little as possible. If you prefer the softer surface that frayed rags produce, choose those with a looser weave that parts easily. But note that the resulting surface may not wear quite as well and that it will probably leave bits on clothing and other furnishings.

Due to the rising costs of all natural fibres, many fabrics are increasingly partly synthetic in origin. As a result, you may find them unpredictable in washing, cutting, fraying and dyeing, so be warned! If you are in doubt, dye a small piece of material first to test for colour and quality.

# Tools and Equipment

There is no great expense involved in equipping yourself for making simple rag rugs. However John Hinchcliffe does give advice on this equipment and also on the more expensive looms which are necessary in weaving rugs

The tools for making rag rugs range from the simplest of implements to complex and often expensive looms with all their accompanying pieces of equipment.

Those necessary for making prodded and hooked rugs depend very much on what you have to hand. Because of the simplicity of the techniques involved, rug makers have always adapted their own tools from what was readily available. Prodded rugs simply require a sharpish implement which will create holes in the base fabric and can then be used to push the rags through to the other side to form loops.

In the past, some people preferred to work with wood, whittling an old peg or carving a suitable length of wood to shape. Others found metal more practical, filing down large nails to a comfortable length, and many people used whatever was available—bones and horns, for example. Like the process itself, such tools earned themselves a wide variety of nicknames such as 'stobber', 'podger', 'pegger', 'bodger' and 'probber'. And they varied not only from one area to another, but from household to household.

Hooked rugs were made on the same principle of inserting rags into a foundation fabric, but the method was rather different. The hook was pushed through the fabric to pick up a loop of the rag strip lying underneath and this was pulled through to the surface. Very simple hooks can be used, though the latchet hooks used for more orthodox rug making are suitable too. Quite mechanical devices were marketed in America and parts of England at the end of the last century, but a home-made hook will serve you just as well, and certainly with less trouble and expense.

There are a variety of ingenious ways of making hooks. A Scottish woman, for instance, recalls having made 'a proper little cleck' (a local term for a hooked rug), with a wooden handle and a sharp hook. Her favourite implement, however, was an old door key filed down to form a hook and point. There are references to one being made from an old fork and another from what appears to be an old smithy hook. This was being put to practical use before World War I and certainly as far back as 1890, and then found favour again

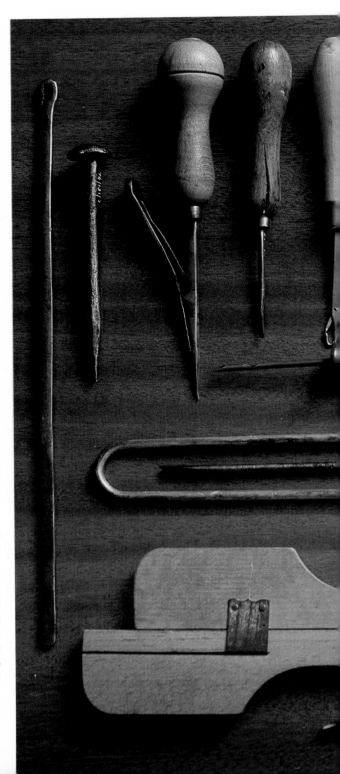

Below: This fascinating collection of tools
has all been used at some time in the past
or present to make rag rugs. They range
from an old meat skewer to a whittled down
clothes peg and a horn. The U-shaped
metal pin in the centre was for cutting strips
of rag into short regular lengths. The large
wooden implement was probably a loop
cutter and the metal pin at the bottom
perhaps a prodder and cutter in combination

during World War II. The owner's materials appeared to change with the times if her hook did not: silk stockings before and during World War I and lisle ones during World War II.

Just as linen and then burlap were used as a base for rugs in the past, you too must decide on a suitable foundation, bearing in mind what is required of it and what is available today. Sacking is increasingly hard to obtain, so hessian or a similarly coarse woven fabric will prove a more readily available choice. It should be flexible, easy to work with and hard wearing. You will also need a long ruler and felt tipped pens or chalk for marking out your design ready for work.

Plaited or braided rugs require only needle and thread for their assembly. An ordinary sewing thread used single or double should prove adequate. If not, experiment with stronger threads until you find the most suitable type. Having made a hook for hooking rugs, you may like to use the same tool for crochet, though any fairly large, ready-made crochet hook will work just as well with rags as with yarn, and often to more interesting and unusual effect.

The choice of needles for rag knitting is simply a matter of ease and individual preference. You may like the feel and warmth of wood, or find that metal slides through the loops of rag more easily. The size you use depends very much on the type of fabric or rag being knitted and the width of the individual strips. You must experiment for a suitable tension and adjust your needle size accordingly. Again you will need a needle and thread to sew the strips together for a continuous length of rag.

Fairly small hooked and prodded rugs can be worked quite satisfactorily on your lap, but if you intend making a large piece or exploring the craft extensively, a frame will keep the foundation fabric taut and the tension even. A large picture frame would prove adequate. You could either tack the foundation fabric to the frame, section by section, rolling areas of completed rug at the front to keep it out of your way, or you can tack webbing along the top and bottom edges of the frame, drilling holes in the sides so that the fabric can be stitched and laced into place. This will also result in a flat, firm surface.

Alternatively, an embroidery frame will serve the same purpose. Such frames are widely available and are generally found in two styles. One type is designed to stand on a table, the other to stand freely on the floor. Both have frames that swivel so that not only can you adjust the angle for working, but you can also turn the work right over to see the back and front without having to turn the frame right round or peer underneath. Some embroidery frames have roller bars so that you can roll on a completed section before starting on the next.

Certainly the cheapest frame would be one you made yourself. Only a few simple carpentry techniques are involved in this. Assemble four

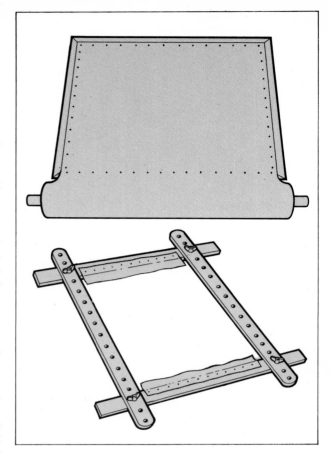

lengths of wood, in pairs of equal length, and mitre or joint the ends to form a rectangular frame. Mount this frame, by means of screws and wing nuts, between two upright supports on a firm common base. This will enable the frame to swing round or be adjusted during working. If your technical knowledge is wider, you may be able to integrate rollers into the design.

It is certainly not necessary for frames, even those meant for simple weaving, to be complicated. One only has to study those used in primitive societies to recognize the simplicity of the basic principles behind the craft, and wonder at the range of textiles produced with a minimum of equipment. It is very easy for the modern weaver, surrounded by sophisticated equipment and aware of the many technicalities of the craft, to forget the creative oppprtunities at his or her fingertips. A weaver is limited only by the size and adaptability of his loom, and it is often surprising how varied his experiments can be. Beginners interested in weaving rag rugs must therefore consider the amount of space available, the money they can afford to spend on the craft and the time they have to spare in deciding where to begin. After all, it is not that much more difficult to work on a floor loom than it is on a table model.

John Hinchcliffe has decided to introduce the craft of weaving with rags with small pieces of tapestry done on a homemade frame. A picture frame would serve equally well, though you will

*Left: It is not only cheaper to make frames for rag rug making yourself, but infinitely more satisfying too. If you know how to handle a saw and make a few basic joints, you should be able to make one with little difficulty. As long as you have a frame that keeps the base fabric under even tension all round, the frame can be as crude or as sophisticated as you like. The two shown here are fairly basic, requiring the minimum of woodworking skills*

*Right: In progressing to weaving rag rugs, put the craft and the amount of equipment it may seem to require into perspective by considering how primitive and particularly nomadic man (the latter having to improvise each time the camp or village moved on) has woven textiles in the past. This photograph shows two Navaho Indian women creating a striped blanket on a loom supported between two tree trunks in the Canyon de Chelly, Arizona, U.S.A.*

need some odd lengths of wood to hold the weft threads apart and to keep the tension even.

To weave any reasonably sized rug you will need a 24-inch (61cm) wide four-shaft table loom. This will also enable you to weave strips or small pieces which can then be sewn together to make larger rugs. A larger loom would be too heavy to move around and would need a permanent home.

Looms of any type can appear alarming, especially when they are being set up ready for weaving. However, as they are all basically set up in the same way, once the process is understood and put into practice, the craft becomes less of a mystery and you can begin to experiment with weaves.

One of the projects in this book shows you how to set up a table loom in detail, and then shows some of the possibilities of weaving with rags. John Hinchcliffe's intention is very much to excite and stimulate the reader into experimenting with the basic techniques in a creative manner. And he is anxious to point out that all the projects in this book are only starting points for the use of rags in rugs—the book offers no hard and fast conclusions, it is not meant to restrain the reader with rules and rigid formulas. The use of rags in weaving is very original and unusual, and worth the effort of learning to understand and use a loom for the first time.

There are four basic types of loom that the craftsman will come across. They are as follows.

**The rigid heddle type of loom.** This is the simplest form of loom, the warp being stretched between two rollers, one at the back and another at the front. Each roller is controlled by a ratchet, enabling the release of the warp as and when it is required, and the adjustment of the tension.

The warp passes through a rigid heddle of wood or metal, and it combines the action of lowering or raising the warp ends to create a shed. The weft can then be passed through the resulting shed. The heddle also enables the weaver to space the warp and it assists in the beating down of the weft to form the woven structure. It very much resembles the reed, but in this type of loom the function of the two are combined, enabling the weaver to work plainweave.

**Two-shaft table loom.** This can only be used for plainweave but it does allow the weaver to work with more ease.

**Four-shaft table loom.** This is the most practical of the looms so far discussed. Any weaver who intends to specialize in rugs need have no larger loom than a four-shaft because it allows great flexibility in spite of its size.

The weaving process is dictated by the threading of the warp through the heddle or healds, which, being attached to the shafts, lifts and lowers the warp in a variety of combinations for different patterns.

35

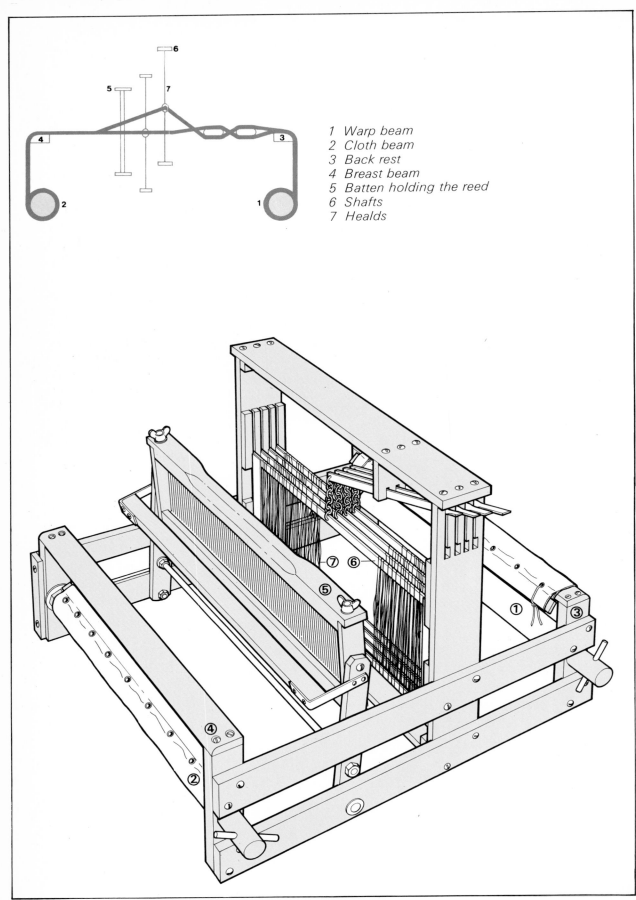

1  Warp beam
2  Cloth beam
3  Back rest
4  Breast beam
5  Batten holding the reed
6  Shafts
7  Healds

*Above: This Scandinavian Countermarch loom is the type John Hinchcliffe would recommend to anyone intending to take up weaving rag rugs in any quantity. Weaving on any type of loom, and a floor loom in particular, is a fairly technical and specialized business. It can also be expensive. If these factors are overcome, the creation of woven rag rugs will prove as satisfying to you as it does to John Hinchcliffe. He introduces the various parts and describes the shedding mechanism of the large floor loom in project 7 on page 88. However a table loom can be bought quite cheaply second-hand, and should prove an ideal starting point for the beginner*

*Left: A detailed drawing of a four-shaft table loom identifies all the working parts enabling you to follow the dressing of the loom in Project 5. The illustration above shows how the warp runs through the loom from the back beam to the front apron*

The four-shaft loom offers the rug weaver more choice in patterned weaving, while there are many specialist techniques that require four shafts. The shafts are manipulated—raised and lowered—either by pressing down or lifting up levers at the side or in the middle of the loom. Each lever is directly attached to a shaft.

This type of loom is available in several sizes but, if faced with a choice, the weaver should select the strongest in frame and narrowest in width. This is because an endless number of strips can be successfully woven to be later sewn together.

**Foot looms.** On such models, the raising and lowering of the shafts controlling the warp threads is worked automatically with the feet by pushing pedals that pivot at the back of the loom. These are known as countermarch or counterbalance looms. John Hinchcliffe prefers using the double countermarch, because it is the better of the two, and recommends that anyone considering the purchase of such a loom chooses one with a batten that is over-slung or hangs from the top of the loom.

The overall advantage of floor looms is their size and strength which allow the weaver to create large pieces that are impossible within the confines of a table model. And traditionally, the best floor looms for general weaving—and especially for rug weaving—come from Scandinavia.

## Tools and Equipment

Basically, weaving is the interlacing of two sets of threads, the warp and the weft. In dress and furnishing fabrics, the warp and weft usually both show. Most rug weaving demands that the weft completely cover and hide the warp, so the latter needs to be very strong and placed on the loom evenly tensioned, but in Sweden the warp is traditionally allowed to show as much as the weft. The weaver must therefore decide which approach to adopt.

As the interlacing of the threads is done for you by the loom, you must decide before considering the purchase of a loom just how serious you are about exploring the craft. You must take into account the type and size of rugs you envisage weaving. All these factors have a direct bearing on the type of loom you choose. Then, when you have decided, buy the very best you can afford, whether a table model or a floor loom. Much of the basic equipment required comes with the loom on purchase, but you may need to supplement it with accessories.

**Reeds.** The reed sits in the batten, spaces the warp threads evenly and beats down the weft. Reeds are available in various sizes and lengths, their size relating to the number of warp threads to the centimetre or inch. The wires in the reeds are known as 'dents', a No. 8 reed having eight dents, a No. 10, ten dents, and so on.

In rug making, reeds that are low in number are most suitable—Nos. 4, 6, 8 and 12, for example. If you are making a rug with four or eight warp ends to the inch or equivalent metric measurement, use a No. 4 reed. For a rug with six to twelve ends per inch, a No. 6 should prove suitable.

**Healds.** Healds are attached to the shafts which control the movement of the warp during the weaving process. They can be made of string, string attached to metal eyes, or solely of wire.

Most table looms have wire healds and metal shafts, but on foot looms, waxed or unwaxed string attached to metal eyes for easy threading and strength allow greater flexibility.

**Hooks.** A flat reed hook enables the weaver to thread the warp ends through the reed. A heald hook performs the same task for the healds. You can, however, thread the reed and the healds by hand, unless the warp is particularly fine.

**Raddle.** This is essential for spacing the warp ends evenly after lifting them off the warping board and transferring them to the back beam of the loom. It enables the weaver to place the warp on the loom to the width of the rug to be woven.

**Warping board.** A warping board is a device for making the warp. Its size depends on the length and size of the warp required.

**Shuttles.** Shuttles carry the yarn or rag weft through the shed with ease and speed. The size of the shuttle you use depends on the width of the rug to be worked, but they are usually made of wood.

**A hand beater.** This is used to beat down the weft in tapestry weaving.

**Skein winder.** These come in various designs, but choose an umbrella type that clamps onto a table if possible. They are useful for unwinding skeins of wool and three will enable you to ply wools together.

**Loom cord.** This strong cord is useful for tying treddles, shafts etc. on the loom.

**Temples.** Temples are adjustable templates that maintain the correct width of the rug while work is in progress.

Finally, there is the subject of the yarns to be used for the warp and weft.

**Warp yarns.** Any warp needs to be strong, and particularly so for rugs. Use linen if possible as this is the strongest, but cotton is very good and especially recommended for tapestry weaving.

**Weft yarns.** Although you will be weaving primarily with rags, you will be using quite a lot of wool, especially at the beginning and end of a rug. You will also be using it in some of the pile techniques outlined later in the book, where rows of woollen plainweave are worked between rows of hand knotted rags, for example.

A 2-ply wool is generally suitable, but it usually has to be plied depending on, and according to, the warp setting of four ends to the inch. However, it is essential to emphasize the importance of experimenting with many yarns in rag weaving— wool, cotton, hair and synthetics.

The basic tools and accessories which you will need when you begin weaving, prodding or braiding rugs from rags are few in number, but as you begin work seriously, you will demand more from your equipment, particularly if you are weaving. When you move onto a floor loom, the range of pieces will expand accordingly. When you buy the loom, either from a shop, a studio or by mail order, you will be able to see at a glance what is available.

1 *Rigid heddle*
2 *Heald hook*
3 *Heald*
4 *Reed*
5 *Raddle*
6 *Reed hook*
7 *Tenterhook or temple*
8 *Boat shuttle*
9 *Stick shuttle*
10 *Skein winder*
11 *Warping board*

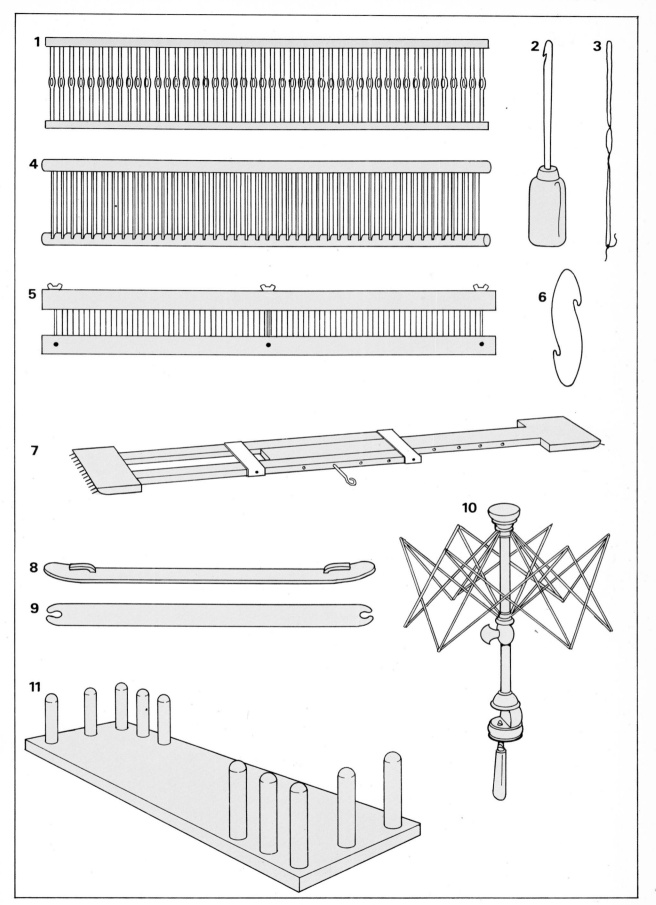

# Project 1: Prodding or Hooking a Rag Rug

The techniques for making rag rugs are different but the end results are much the same—it is up to you to decide which method you prefer and then experiment with dyed and undyed rags for a variety of looped and cut pile effects. The equipment is minimal; the rags should cost you nothing at all

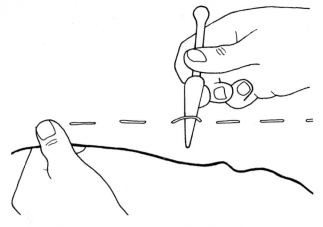

If your base fabric is irregular in shape, the easiest way to establish the run of the grain or the direction of the warp and weft threads is to draw out a thread on each side to form a regularly shaped rectangle. Alternatively, if you intend working a small rug on your lap, the lifting of a thread around all four sides will indicate where you can turn under the edge to begin work.

Place your fabric on a flat surface. Then with a long ruler and chalk or a felt-tipped pen, begin to draw out your design. Measure its length and breadth accurately, making sure you follow the straight of the grain. Leave a reasonable allowance around the edges for turning in. Finally, fill the area of the rug with a simple design.

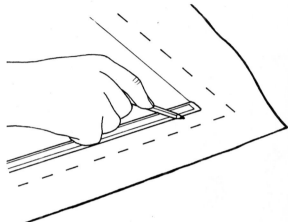

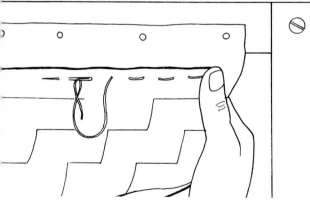

If your work area is limited and the rug you intend working fairly small, a frame will be unnecessary. If you prefer working on an evenly tensioned surface, mount the base fabric into the frame. Most have a length of tape tacked along the top edge, so turn in the border of the base fabric and stitch firmly in place. Repeat along the bottom edge or roll the excess fabric around the bottom bar and tack down securely.

Left: Though the novice rug maker would be well advised to begin with simple designs, inspiration and confidence can be drawn from this huge rug designed in 1925 by the English artist William Nicholson. It incorporates all the signs of the zodiac. An acquisition of the Victoria and Albert Museum in London, it is faded but closer inspection of the pile reveals that the original colours must have been very bright indeed

You will need base fabric to the size of the desired rug. This can be of any coarsely woven fabric, the threads of which can be parted easily with either a hook or prodding tool. Hessian is probably the most suitable and easily available, though in the past sacking was simple to obtain and very hard wearing too.

A prodder or hooking tool can be picked up in junk shops or antique markets, or perhaps passed down within a family.

For rags use cotton, wool or synthetics. Be well advised not to mix them until you are experienced in handling various fibres. Differences in weight and texture can often cause stretching and give an undesired effect.

Prodding is perhaps the easiest of the techniques, though exponents of hooking may disagree. If working on your lap, begin by turning in the top edge by about 2.5cm (1in). Hold the folded edge in your left hand (if right-handed), the prodder in your right. Push the prodder into and through both layers, approximately 2.5cm (1in) in from the left edge.

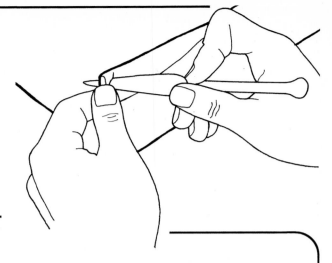

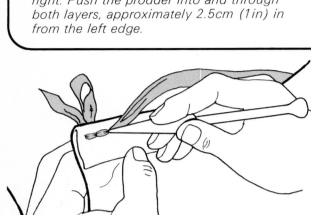

Cut a length of rag, either on the straight or on the bias. Push the end through the hole formed with the tool. Make a second hole in the same way a little further on, then push the rag through to form a loop on the other side. Note that you are working from the wrong side. Repeat along the edge until the strip of rag is used up. Then start with another.

After a while you will see the loops forming on the right side, while a line resembling a close backstitch lies on the wrong side facing you. Make sure the loops are fairly regularly spaced and that they are of equal length. When you reach the end of the row, start again, working through one layer of fabric instead of two.

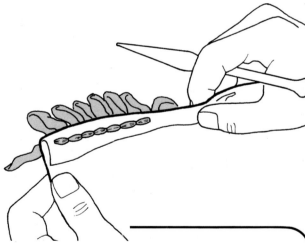

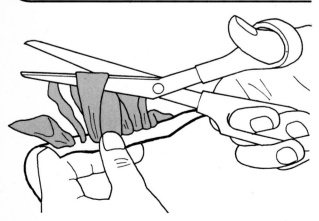

As each line is completed, turn the rug over and slide the blades of the scissors into each loop. Pull taut and cut neatly. Bias cut strips will result in a more uneven pile while straight cut rags provide a more evenly textured surface.

*Below: John Hinchcliffe here demonstrates how to prod a small rug on a frame with multi-coloured undyed cotton rags. He is working from the back or underside of the rug and following the lines of the simple stepped design from left to right*

*Left: Here is the completed rug, seen from the right side after all the loops have been cut. The rug requires the edges turning in to be quite finished. A backing will prevent excessive wear*

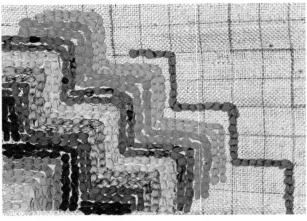

*Top: This sample incorporates dyed rags into a rug. The resulting pile is more positive, the colours are easily distinguishable in relation both to the design and to one another*

*Bottom: This small detail shows the back of the same sample*

Both hooking and prodding are very easy techniques to learn and to put to immediate and practical use. The resulting pile is almost identical in effect; it is only the methods that are different, though prodding is more flexible in that it can be worked on the lap or mounted on a frame. As hooking requires a tensioned surface, it is nearly always worked on a frame of some kind, thus enabling the rug maker to work with speed and facility. Turn back to page 34 for further information about frames and for illustrations and instructions on how to build your own.

Although John Hinchcliffe only demonstrates prodding in this first project, all the rugs and samples illustrated could have been hooked just as easily. Whereas in prodding, the rug maker works from the wrong side, pushing the rag through the base fabric to the right side to form loops, hooking involves working from the right side with the rag strip lying underneath and being guided by the left hand (if right-handed), while the right hand operates the hook, pushing it through the base, catching the rag in the hook and pulling it through to the right side. Most exponents of hooking admit it is slower than prodding, but prefer to have the more immediate control of being able to see the pattern evolving in front of them rather than having to keep turning over the rug to see the progress of the pile and design. Experiment with both techniques first of all, and make your own decision.

Although cut pile rugs have always been popular in Great Britain, American rug makers rarely cut the loops of their hooked and prodded rugs. This may be due to the fact that English rugs were always created for practical rather than aesthetic purposes, the design being secondary to the warmth and comfort of the pile provided. Certainly, when the loops are cut, any patterning becomes less distinct. And this may well be the reason why the Americans preferred to leave the pile uncut, their charming and often highly complex designs thus being clearly defined for all to see.

Prodding uncut pile is certainly the quickest way to work a rug, and if using a fairly thick fabric such as a soft, loosely woven wool, a design will work up in no time at all. The two rugs illustrated on the following pages indicate two very different approaches: one is cotton cut into very fine strips and worked into a small mat with a clear pictorial theme; the other is a large woollen rug that is not only dark and dramatic in its colouring, but worked in rather a haphazard fashion. Both are effective.

Having decided therefore upon the technique to be employed—hooking or prodding—and taking practical considerations into account such as whether the rug will receive a great deal of wear in which case the rags selected should be easy to clean, colour fast and hard wearing, or purely for decorative purposes in which case such factors are less relevant, you should draw out your design on the base fabric.

If you are unsure of your artistic abilities, begin with something simple yet effective. Try a single motif in the centre and contain it within a border around the edge. Geometric patterns require less drawing skill, and you can use everyday objects from around the house if you lack the confidence to work freehand. Use plates for circles, books for squares and rectangles, or kitchen utensils for more unusual shapes. Repeat the motifs for borders, or overlap them for interesting variations of the basic shape. Alternatively, use a ruler for vertical, horizontal or diagonal stripes, stepped designs such as the one being worked by John Hinchcliffe on page 43, or create regular or irregular grids.

If, at the beginning, you feel your artistic abilities are inadequate, if only through lack of confidence, then keep a scrapbook of ideas from magazines, pieces of wallpaper and wrapping paper for reference. Use it as a jotter for any ideas that come to mind.

A simple ploy which will increase your awareness of shape and design even further is to cut out a square of plain or coloured paper, and then to cut these into various pieces—like a jig-saw, but with straight rather than interlocking edges. Play around with this within a drawn square to the same size so that the shapes balance one another. It is, after all, a skill to be learnt like any other craft, even if you have no experience of designing.

*Below: Cut pile rugs have always been highly favoured in the north of England, where this fine specimen was made and is now on display in the Folk Museum of West Yorkshire, Halifax. Its bright colouring and bold geometric design are typical of rugs hooked and prodded in the area, as is the thick shaggy pile*

If narrative themes appeal more, begin by sketching in the shapes and figures so that you can balance the overall design, and then fill in detail later as you work. Indulge yourself in uninhibited visions and perspectives, be bold and unconventional in your use of colour, try not to become too serious and allow an element of humour to creep in wherever it seems natural to do so. Above all, employ invention and broad artistic licence in your compositions. The results will surprise and reward you. Perhaps like the nurse who travelled in the mission boat pictured above, you can draw your inspiration from your own activities. Employ twentieth-century images or perhaps copy scenes from paintings.

*Above: The maker of this small cotton rug did not draw out her design first, but simply hooked it as she went along. She was one of a colony of English immigrants living in Labrador, Canada, who were taught the craft at the Grenfell Mission where rug making was encouraged as a cottage industry. The picture shows the local mission boat*

Below: A strikingly patterned English prodded rug worked in a random fashion and all in wool on sacking. The small detail at the bottom left shows the back of the same rug

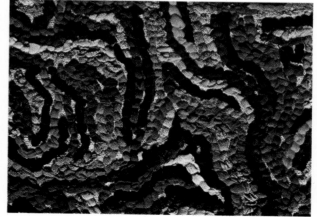

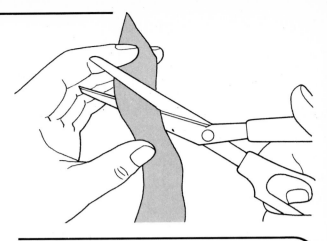

An alternative to working with long strips of bias cut rag is to cut rags into short pieces and insert them individually for an even more luxuriant pile. By cutting the strips diagonally across, the pieces are slightly pointed at each end and so create an interestingly textured but less even surface.

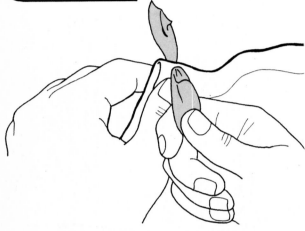

Fold the base fabric, wrong sides facing, so that the folded edge is uppermost and towards you. Pierce through both layers with the prodding tool. Push a strip through, and then check that it is of equal length each side of the fold, adjusting as shown here. Repeat all along the fold.

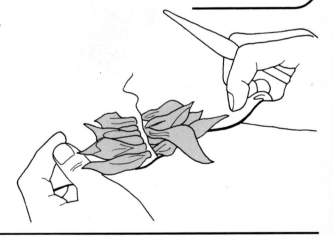

Hold the fabric each side of the fold and pull so that the fold opens and the rags lie each side. Make another fold a little way from the first and begin again. Work the lines close together for a firm pile, or space them further apart for a looser textural effect.

Already you have a wide range of exciting possibilities at your fingertips. You can hook or prod your rug; insert long or individual strips of rag; work in cotton, wool, silk, or synthetics, or combine them; use undyed rags, dyed rags, or the two together; insert them close together for a firm upright pile, or further apart for a more open and flexible one; you can create boldly patterned rugs, rugs that tell a tale, or rugs that simply keep you warm.

Create them as John Hinchcliffe does, with an uninhibited enthusiasm for the raw materials and with an awareness of the potential within the limitations of the techniques at hand. Mix, as he does, sound commonsense with flair and style.

Rely on your own instinct for what looks right for you, just as he does. Treat your rags as a painter would use a paint palette. Display your talents by not only combining colours, but creating them with the help of dyes. As a result you will be able to achieve a number of variations of one colour, thus allowing you to have the freedom to create striated backgrounds. Areas of static colour tend to look dead, lacking vitality and depth, so avoid playing safe. The more adventurous you are, the more exciting the visual results.

Although it is always difficult to achieve the finest results at first, persevere. It is wiser to begin with small samples until you have mastered the basic techniques.

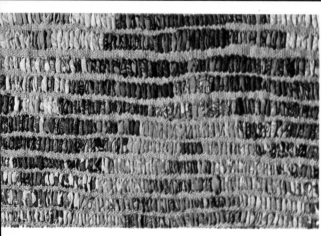

Above: Direct dyes were used to dye the
rags in parts of this thick cotton rug,
each strip of which was inserted individually.
The design is a variation on the zigzag
using simple straight lines. The underside
or back of the rug is in complete contrast
to the top surface, as this detail on the left
indicates

# Project 2: Plaiting or Braiding a Rug

John Hinchcliffe suggests various ideas for assembling attractive rugs from plaited or braided rags. The technique is certainly the oldest of the more homespun methods of making floor covering, there being references to rugs of this type in use as early as the eighteenth century

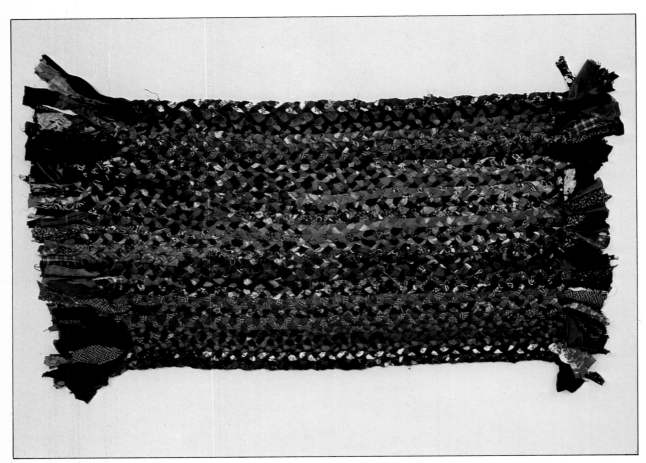

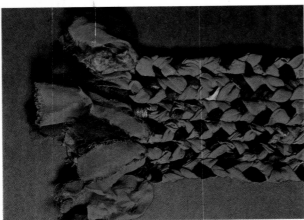

*Above: John Hinchcliffe feels it is important to apply each technique to different fabrics, testing for durability, texture and appearance. This large rug consists of heavy, undyed woollen braids assembled adjacent to one another, the ends being left free to form a luxuriant fringe*

*Left: In contrast, a sample braid of pure silk chiffon, the fabrics dyed to exotic effect*

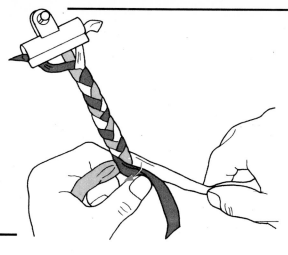

*Having cut three strips of rag to equal width, secure them at one end—either tied to a chair, a door handle, or on a firm surface with a nail and clip as shown here. The object is to interlace the strands by hand under tension. Work from the outside inwards, beginning with the right-hand strip. Lift it over the central strand into the middle.*

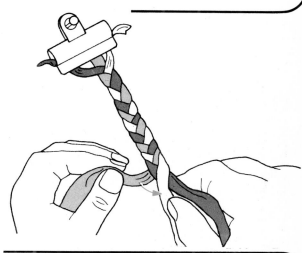

*Next lift the strand on the left over the strip now lying in the middle. Finally, take the orginal centre strand that now lies on the right into the middle. All three strips have now taken up new positions. Continue lifting right over left and left over right to form the plait or braid.*

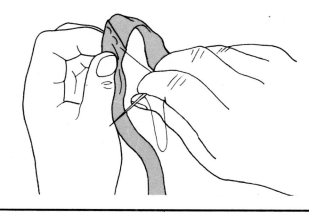

*When you run out of rag, simply sew another into place with needle and thread used singly or double. Work either a close running stitch or a firm backstitch, depending on the fabric in use.*

To plait a rug you will need dyes, rags, needle and thread. Throughout history, men and women have plaited and braided their hair to practical and decorative effect. It seems natural therefore to extend the technique to rug making, simply substituting strips of rag for handfuls of hair and interlacing them for strength and neatness.

Rags can be cut on the straight or bias, but the former will result in firm plaits, the latter in braids that are flexible, almost elastic. Experiment to see for yourself.

For a smooth surface, twist the strips as you work so that the raw edges are hidden within the braid. Those who prefer a more textured surface can leave the edges on show, but be warned that

fraying can occur, especially with really loosely woven fabrics.

Rectangular rugs are the easiest to assemble. Create a number of plaits of equal length. For straight sided rugs, sew the ends back into the plaits neatly; if fringing is preferred, leave the ends free and stitch the strands together where the plaiting finishes. Lay the plaits side by side and then rearrange them until you are pleased with the overall design.

Experiment with different fabrics and colours. Plait strands in three different colours, or work with two in one colour and a third that either darkens or lightens the rug. Use plains and patterns, together or separately.

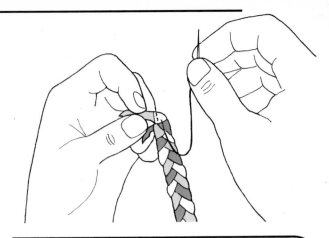

To begin a round rug, work a long plait and then turn in the ends neatly. Check that they are completely hidden within the braid, then sew in place firmly but invisibly. Use whichever stitch seems appropriate, and a thread to match the fabrics.

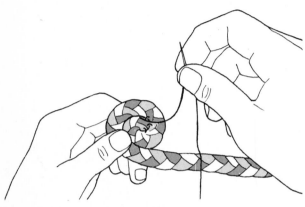

Form the end of the plait into a tight circle and stitch together. Use a slip hem stitch or the tent stitch illustrated. Continue sewing the plait round and round, catching it in place at regular intervals and knotting each time for strength. Do not sew too tightly or the rug will buckle: the only problem in creating a circular rug is in keeping it quite flat. Remember to choose a strong thread and a sharp long needle.

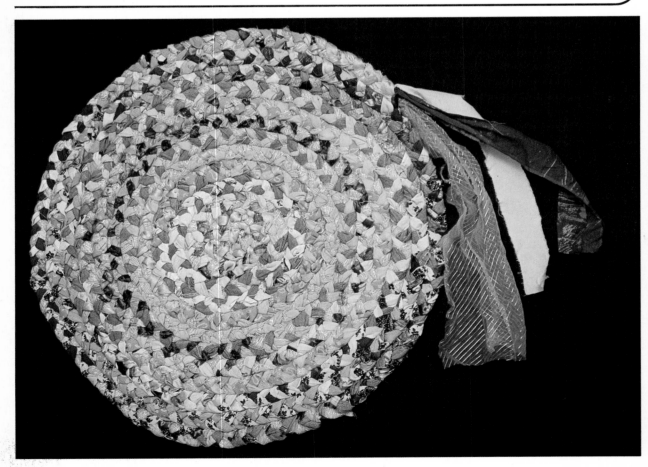

There are any number of alternatives to laying braids adjacent to one another. Round rugs are easy to make and most effective, while circular motifs can be mixed with straight lengths to give an interesting effect. Try stitching braids into triangles, diamonds and rectangles or spirals: they can all be sewn together in various permutations. Alternatively, use plaits as borders for prodded and hooked rugs. Or decorate plaited rugs with embroidery or appliqué as many American rug makers did.

There really are an endless range of possibilities, as the rugs which John Hinchcliffe has made for this project illustrate. They can then be used in any room in the house.

*Left: A half completed round rug that incorporates a range of decorative fabrics—cottons, chintzes, silks and gauzes, shot with gold and silver, and satins. They are all predominantly pale in colour, the resulting plaited 'fabric' displaying a deceptive fragility and delicacy*

*Below: A bold yet pretty rug in dyed and undyed cottons. Small circular motifs are secured within borders of plaits sewn next to one another*

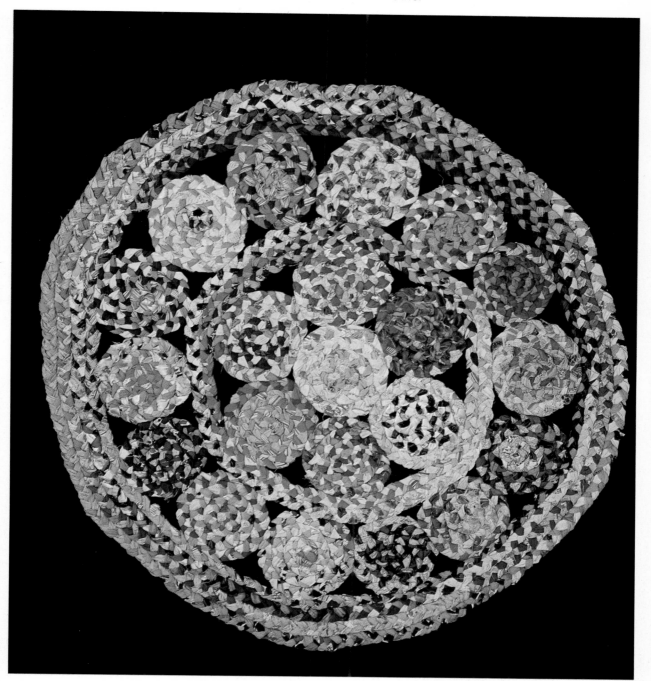

# Project 3: Knitting a Rug

Knitting with lengths of rag instead of yarn is full of interesting possibilities. John Hinchcliffe not only shows you how to get started, work garter stitch and cast off, but he offers ideas for using the technique for plain, patterned and pile rugs

For this project you will need dyed and undyed strips of rag. Prepare them beforehand, sewing them together by hand or machine. Wind them into balls as with ordinary knitting yarn so that they do not become tangled and difficult to use.

The coarser the fabric and the wider the strips, the larger your knitting needles will need to be. Wooden needles are nice to use and ideal for lightweight fabrics, but metal ones allow the loops to slide from one needle to another with greater facility. Try both and decide which you find the easier to handle. Choose needles with a knob at one end: these will prevent the knitting sliding off. You will also need needle and thread for sewing the rags together.

*Left: You might like to begin by knitting some sample lengths to test not only your expertise, but the effect of using different fabrics with needles of varying sizes. This example in undyed bias cut strips of cotton rag is worked in random stripes*

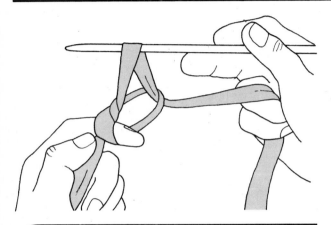

*With the free end of the rag 'yarn' in your left hand, form it into a circle and draw the strip through to form a slip loop. Insert a needle into this loop and transfer it to your left hand. You can now begin casting on. If you are left-handed, work in reverse.*

*It is usual to tension yarn in knitting by looping it around the fingers of the hand controlling the yarn. When working with strips of rag and large needles however, this is often not possible. So with the rag strip in your right-hand, insert the right-hand needle into the loop and take the strip of rag under and over the point of the right-hand needle as indicated by the arrow.*

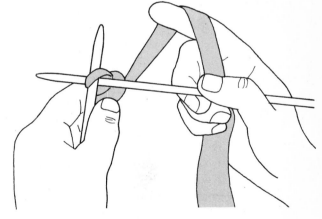

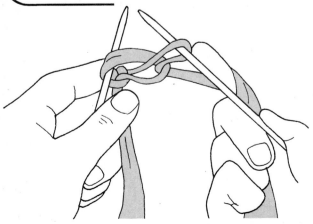

*Draw a new loop through the first and twist to transfer it to the left-hand needle. Place the point of the right-hand needle between the two loops on your left-hand needle, take the rag strip under and over the point as before, draw through a new loop and pass it onto the left-hand needle. Continue until you have the correct number of stitches on the needle.*

*Having cast on the required number of stitches, begin by learning how to work garter stitch, otherwise known as plain knitting. With the needle bearing the stitches in your left hand (if right-handed), insert the tip of the right-hand needle into a loop on your left-hand needle. Take the rag yarn around the back of the right-hand needle as shown.*

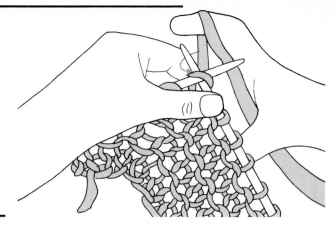

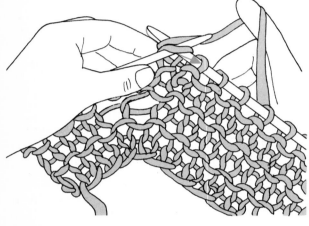

*Bring the point of the needle bearing the rag yarn through the loop on the left-hand needle so that a new stitch is created on the right-hand needle.*

*To complete the new stitch, pull the right-hand needle bearing the new loop off the left-hand needle. Repeat all along the row. You now have some completed new stitche on your right-hand needle. When you have knitted all the stitches, transfer the right-hand needle to your left hand and begin again.*

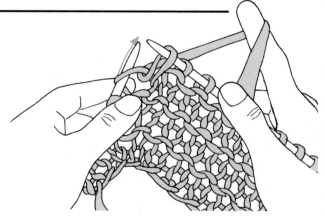

If you intend knitting only a few experimental samples, the tension of each piece will be relatively unimportant. But if you want to knit a rug or series of strips to a given measurement for a planned design, you will need to work a tension square to estimate the correct number of stitches to the centimetre or inch.

If it works out, when using a needle of a particular size with fabric of a certain weight and a measured width, that there are two stitches and two rows to the inch or equivalent metric measure, you will know to cast on twenty-four stitches and work the same number of rows for a knitted piece twelve inches square.

However this will alter with each new fabric or any change in the size of the needle. And it is no good trying to cut corners by estimating the final size of the piece by the width of the stitches cast at random onto your needle. This never reflects an accurate picture. In casting on you are simply creating a firm edge; the finished piece of knitting will be much wider.

Begin as John Hinchcliffe did, by working small samples of plain knitting in strips of cotton rag. By changing from one print to another you can create stripes of different pattern and colour, sewing the ends together at the beginning of a new row. After creating a number of regular or irregular squares or rectangles in this way, consider sewing them together for a larger area in the

*Left: As a simple experiment, John Hinchcliffe has alternated dyed and undyed stripes in two narrow knitted strips and then sewn them together to show how a fairly random pattern can soon develop. The piece is effective in the same way as patchwork*

same way as a piece of patchwork is assembled. This is perhaps the advisable way to start creating knitted rag rugs.

If you feel more ambitious, you could try working pieces in all plain or all patterned fabric; all dyed or all undyed; or mixing them together and arranging the pieces in various geometric permutations: chessboards, zigzags, diagonal steps, ziggurats or stepped pyramids, for optical effects and illusions.

Working individual squares is easy, but how much faster to work long strips and then sew these together either widthways or lengthways. This is a traditional method of creating woven rag rugs, but it can be applied to knitting with equal success.

Working in strips does mean that there needs to be more preparatory work in designing a rug. The best way is to draft a plan of the envisaged design, filling in the various areas with paint, crayons and small clippings of suitable fabric. The next stage is to sort the rags into colours and shades with reference to the plan and then to dye any that do not fit in with the colour pattern. Those of you who have knitted for some time can experiment with simple patterning and motif knitting for additional interest.

John Hinchcliffe is also anxious to explore the potential of knitted pile rugs. The simplest method is to knot lengths of rag together as you work. Then, as each knot is worked into the knitting, push it through to one side. The method is certainly quick but such a rug might be a little disconcerting to walk on in anything less than climbing boots.

Rug makers have experimented with knitted (and crocheted) rags over the years, as history well documents. As a result, John Hinchcliffe found his pieces particularly interesting to make, seeing possibilities not only in rug making, but in knitted rag rugs and covers, fashion accessories such as belts, hats, bags, and fashion garments themselves.

While the historical development of the use of rags in craft work was being investigated for this book, various instances came to light of attempts to hook, prod and even knit short or long lengths

*To cast off, knit the first two stitches in the row and then lift the first over the second with the point of the left-hand needle. Knit another stitch and lift the second over the third. Repeat until only one stitch remains. Cut the rag to leave a long tail for sewing in, then draw this through the loop of the last stitch. Pull tight to finish.*

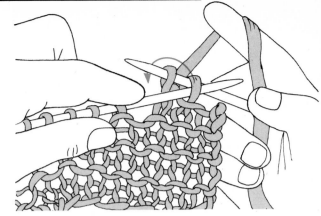

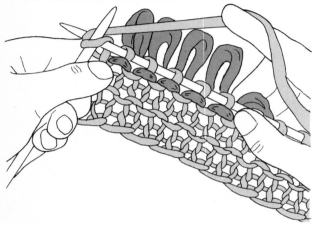

*For a looped or cut pile rug, prepare your rags into strips. Knit one stitch, then insert the end between the two needles. Knit another stitch and pass the strip around it and through to the right side again. Knit a third stitch, leave a loop on the right side and bring the rag through again. Repeat to the end of the row.*

*Alternatively, you can insert the strips individually. Cut a length of rag into small pieces as for the prodded or hooked technique on page 48, and then insert into the knitting in the same way. This method creates a cut pile, whereas the first can be cut or left looped.*

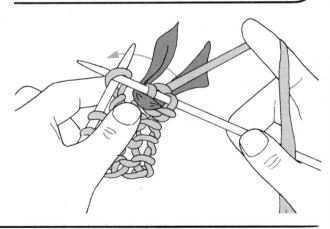

of rag into a knitted base. According to documented evidence, this base was never of rag but another material altogether: string, binder twine, waste yarn or wool.

What intrigues John Hinchcliffe is the similarity between the techniques used in working rags into a knitted base and those he has developed for his own woven rugs. In both cases, long or short strips of rag are inserted into the work, the firmness and tension of the interlaced threads holding the rag pile firmly in place.

Depending on the type of pile preferred—even or uneven, loose or upright and firm—try working one row of rag to one row of knitting, remembering to insert them between alternate stitches on alternate rows for an even distribution of rags all over the surface. Inserting them between the same stitches of alternate rows could result in a striped pile with strips of knitting showing in between.

For an even length of pile, check that the loops or lengths of rag being left on the surface of the rug are equal in height. When the piece is finished and cast off, you can go over the surface more thoroughly, using the point of a needle or a hook to adjust errant strips from the back, if and when necessary.

Such experiments have an obvious application to knitwear in general, and more particularly in fashion. Try a simple waistcoat knitted up in the

yarn stated in the pattern, but with rags inserted all over or to give sporadic effect. Such a garment would not only look unusual but be warm yet light to wear.

A more advanced step would be to work out a planned design in rags. It would be just as easy to introduce stripes, patterns and motifs as in the hooked and prodded rugs in project 1. You could leave the rags looped, or cut them, as preferred. And as with all the projects, work with undyed and dyed rags.

Another idea is to work rags into knitting at intervals. You could work them in singly to resemble bows or ribbons, play with regular or irregular groups of plain or multicoloured rags, or insert the occasional stripe or motif for textural interest. Mix different types of fabric or try altering the height of the pile for a full range of exciting possibilities. Certainly knitting with rags is an attractive proposition and one that could be extended into crochet in a similar way. All you would have to do is use lengths of rag and a crochet hook working in rows or in the round in the usual way. If anything, the technique results in an even firmer textured fabric, though lacking the obvious elasticity of knitting, and does look very attractive whether worked in rag strips or in a quite random manner. The only problem you may come across is in keeping the rags flat but this will depend on the evenness of your tension which is the most important technique to be mastered by any knitter.

*Top: John Hinchcliffe mixed dyed and undyed cotton rags for random stripes in this example of rags inserted into a knitted base. The yarn is a thick string-like cotton that is light and easy to work with. From the back, you can clearly see how the rags have been inserted between alternate stitches on alternate rows*

*Bottom: From the front, a thick luxuriant cotton pile is revealed, covering the knitted base completely*

# Project 4: Weaving Tapestry on a Frame

Tapestry weaving is an ancient technique that requires only a simple frame and nimble fingers. John Hinchcliffe shows you how to prepare the frame ready for working, weaves a number of small pieces and offers ideas for more advanced projects

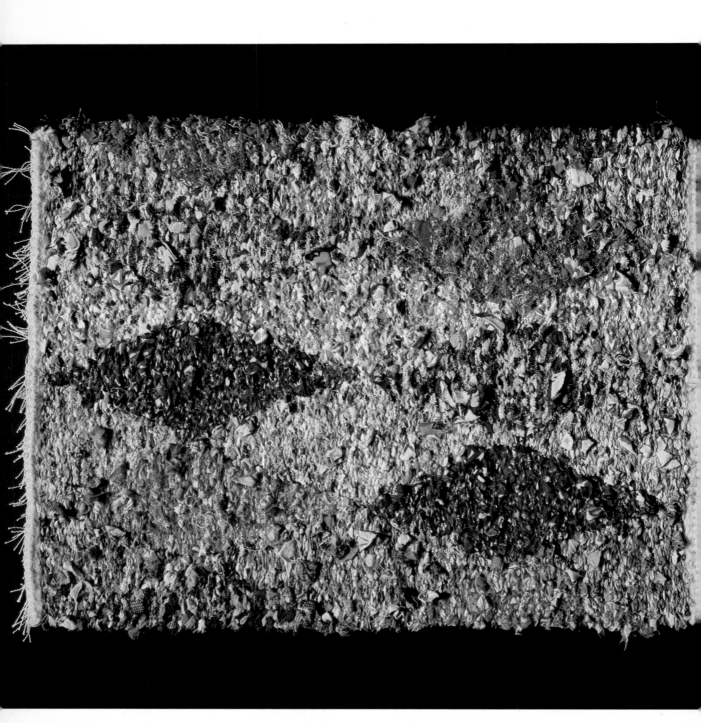

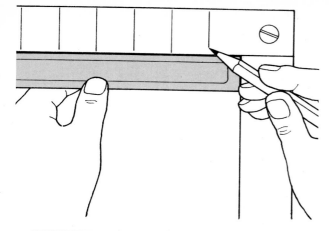

Make or buy a simple frame and then mark the centre of the top and bottom with pen or pencil. Measure outwards each side of this line in either inches or centimetres for a tapestry 40.5cm (16in) wide. You are now ready to wind on the warp with the correct number of threads to the inch or centimetre, in this case four to the inch. Choose a strong cotton warp yarn in readiness for this.

Tie the free end of the warp yarn around the top bar to the left of the left-hand side outer marking. Take the yarn down and through the frame. This is the first warp thread that is used as a guideline for the selvedge of the tapestry weave. Wind up and through and over the frame in a figure of eight movement. Each complete figure will result in two warp threads. Repeat across the frame, then wind one as a guideline for the other selvedge and tie as at the beginning.

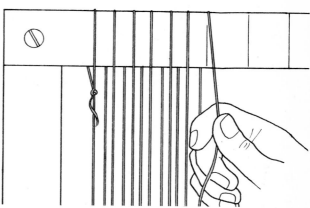

You will need dyed and undyed rags. Prepare them in the usual way, cut into long strips of equal width. Depending on the size of the piece to be woven, you can either use a suitable frame loom which comes to hand (an old picture frame, for instance), or make one yourself. For rugs, you will either be working small pieces which can be sewn together as described in Project 3, or working long strips for assembly in the traditional manner. A frame that measures two and a half times the width should prove adequate in both these cases. Use seasoned timber measuring 5cm (2in) by 2.5cm (1in), and either dovetail the corners or simply screw them together. As long as the frame is strong, its construction is not really important. There is further information on frames on page 34.

You will also need three additional lengths of the same timber, they are called cross sticks and are for tensioning and separating the warp and creating a shed. 'Shed' is the term used in weaving to describe the space created in the warp when the ends (the threads that make up the warp) are separated, either by the insertion of cross sticks or by the lifting or lowering of shafts. The shuttle carrying the weft is passed through the shed in one direction or another.

*Left: This subtly coloured piece of tapestry is built up of regular diamond shaped motifs. It combines ready patterned rags with those dyed with indigo*

You will need some cotton warp yarn which is strong and especially suitable for weaving with rags; a tapestry bobbin wound with soft cotton yarn for working the beginning and end of the tapestry; a fork beater for beating down the weft; and a large curved carpet needle for sewing in the warp ends. All these items can be purchased in large stores or specialist shops.

Although many examples of woven tapestry appear to be very intricate, this apparent complexity is deceptive. Tapestry is, in fact, the easiest of all the weaving techniques and John Hinchcliffe recommends it as your first weaving project not only because of the small amount of equipment required, but because the actual process of weaving rags with the fingers helps give a clear understanding of what the craft is about.

Tapestry is concerned with the most fundamental construction of threads, the interlacing of warp and weft known as plainweave. But whereas in most woven fabrics this construction is based on a balanced distribution of the warp and weft, tapestry involves an off-balance apportionment with the weft covering a widely spaced warp.

The pattern or ornamentation is built up in individual areas, each one being woven with its own coloured weft. In the weaving of ordinary patterns on a loom, the weft passes from one selvedge to the other and back again, the pattern being controlled by the way in which the warp is threaded through the healds on the shafts and the

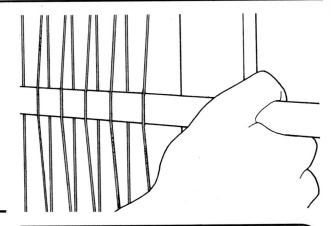

Insert the first cross stick into the warp, *working* under *the first thread and* over *the next.* When the cross stick is in position across the full width of the warp, move it up to the top of the frame.

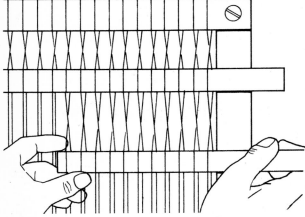

Insert the second stick working in reverse, over *the first thread and* under *the second* so that a cross is formed in the warp. In this way a shed is created. Push this stick to the top too. If holes are drilled in the ends of these sticks, they can be tied loosely together. Turn the frame upside down and insert a third stick. Work this under *the first thread and* over *the second.* Another cross will be formed.

Using the yarn wound onto the bobbin, tie the free end around the right-hand side of the frame just above the two cross sticks at the bottom. Weave in and out with the bobbin, then cut the yarn and tie the other end around the left-hand side of the frame. This thread forms the lower edge of your tapestry.

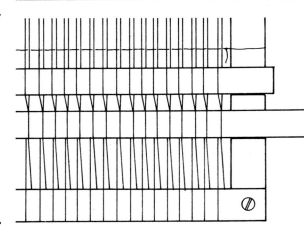

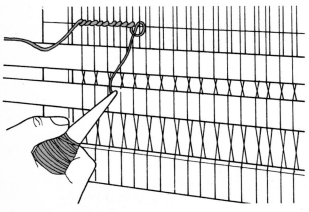

Work a row of Soumack stitch along this thread. To do this tie the yarn on the bobbin to the first warp thread on the left-hand side, then take the bobbin forward around the back of the thread and to the front. Repeat all along the warp as shown, and then work back across the threads in the opposite direction. Try to keep the stitches as even as possible.

sequence in which these are raised and lowered.

In traditional tapestry it is rare for a single weft to run from selvedge to selvedge, it being far more usual for a piece to be built up of a number of discontinuous wefts spanning the width of the weave and moving in opposite directions.

This method of building up a design with large and small areas of differently coloured wefts allows the weaver great freedom of expression, the intricacy and balance of the pattern or picture being dependant on the individual's skill and inherent sense of design rather than technical prowess with the loom.

There are various tapestry techniques, but the one John Hinchcliffe demonstrates is the oldest and most traditional. It is known as Kelim and in it the areas of the weft are woven so independently of one another that small selvedges are created, leaving tiny slits in the fabric. If small and woven correctly, these do not show in the finished piece, but if rather long or carelessly woven they can be sewn up on completion of the piece. The diagram on page 65 shows the formation of these slits clearly.

The purist tapestry weaver will always employ the traditional technique of Kelim, so suitable for hard edged geometric designs. The weaver will base all patterning on a grid system, allowing for a high degree of flexibility within this rigid format. A careful scrutiny of many old rugs will reveal that they have been made by the Kelim method, though the amount of detail within their designs might initially have misled you into thinking otherwise.

There are additional techniques allied to Kelim. Soumack, for instance, which involves wrapping the weft around the warp ends. This is briefly described on pages 62 and 75 in the section on finishing rugs. There are various methods of knotting into the weave to produce a pile. Those of you who want to explore these are advised to read books specializing in the subject, or to study these rugs at close quarters in museums, specialist shops and import warehouses which often stock Kelims in quantity.

Working a tapestry by the Kelim or slit method is very easy once the loom is set up and warped, and the basis of the technique understood. In practice, the only problem a complete beginner might have is in keeping the outer edges of the woven fabric straight, and the small selvedges within the piece parallel to one another. Overcoming this is simply a matter of controlling the weaving of the weft for an even tension as you work from one side to another.

John Hinchcliffe recommends leaving the outer warp thread on each side unwoven, using it as a guideline for keeping the edges as straight as possible. An alternative is to use the two outer warp threads on each side as your selvedge and take the weft around them twice instead of once. This helps adjust the level and makes for stronger edges at the same time.

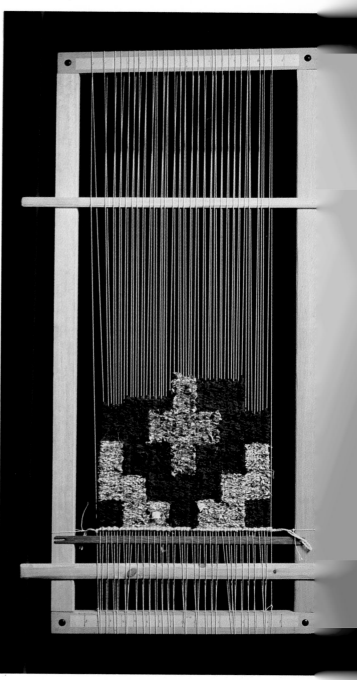

*Below: John Hinchcliffe made this simple frame loom with its three cross sticks from odd pieces of wood in his studio. The piece of tapestry on the loom is woven with cotton rags—an undyed pink which contrasts well with a rich dark blue obtained with indigo dye. The design is in symmetrically stepped lines, a hard edged pattern that involves using the Kelim or slit technique*

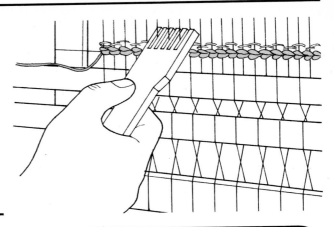

*On the completion of the second row of Soumack stitch, weave two rows of plain-weave, working under one warp thread and over the next. The second row is woven under and over alternate threads to those in the first. As you finish each row, beat it down with the fork for an even fabric.*

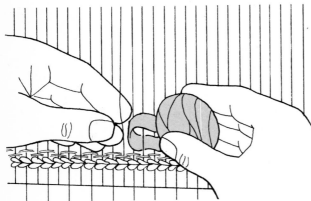

*If working to a drawn out design planned to scale, pin this behind your frame so that you can see which areas to weave in which colour. If you are working a random pattern of your own design, this will not be necessary. Begin weaving your first section. Roll the rag into a neat ball and then begin to weave under and over each thread, using your fingers to carry the yarn through the warp.*

The creation of any tapestry consists of several quite separate stages, the first of which is the acquisition of a frame. A small disused picture frame would be suitable for any experimental pieces, but if you want to weave quite large strips for making up into even larger rag rugs, then you will obviously need something larger and stronger. It is not a good idea to try working on anything too large otherwise the frame will be very unwieldy, especially in domestic surroundings.

If you have no four-sided frame available and are against the idea of investing in one until you have established a mastery of the technique, look around the house or garden for a means of improvization. There are many possibilities but do remember, the size of your frame will determine the size of the piece being woven.

The frame can be warped in several ways. John Hinchcliffe finds that wrapping the warp around the frame is quick and very easy, and it certainly does not seem to limit the ease with which he can weave. Other weavers prefer to insert two rows of nails into the top and bottom bar of the frame, spacing them regularly 2.5cm (1in) apart and alternately positioned one below the other. These, they claim, hold the warp more securely; there is less likelihood that they cross over one another; and the tension is more reliable.

Any warp must be carefully spaced. Decide how wide your piece of tapestry is to be, work out the number of ends to each inch or equivalent metric measurement, and then wind the warp yarn around the frame in a figure of eight movement. Check that none of the ends crosses over another. Test the tension with the flat of your hand. It should be comfortably taut. Tighten any ends that seem slack by distributing the excess across the entire warp. Alternatively pad with pieces of folded fabric or paper inserted between the errant warp end and the top or bottom bar, whichever is easier.

The next steps have been covered in detail in the step-by-step drawings, but remember to insert the cross sticks to create the shed. This will not be a very wide opening but will certainly help in weaving the weft through the warp. After tying on the thread that will form the lower edge of your piece of tapestry, work two rows of Soumack stitch and two of plainweave. You are now ready to begin weaving your design with strips of dyed and undyed rag. Plainweave is described in detail on the next page.

To finish a piece, work as at the beginning but in reverse. Work two rows of plainweave in soft cotton yarn, then secure the warp ends with two rows of Soumack.

Before you cut across the warp to release the piece from the frame, decide how you want to finish the ends. If you are intending to patchwork a number of pieces together, cut the warp fairly short for sewing back into the fabric of the weave. If you have woven longer strips for sewing

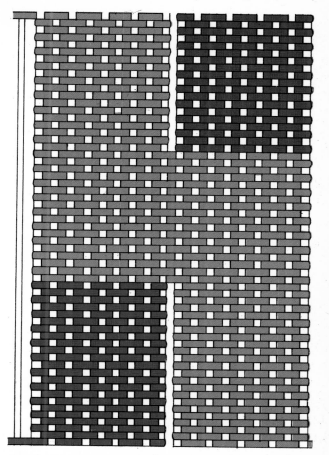

*Right: The illustration at the top shows the detail of the tapestry directly below in diagrammatic form. The two differently coloured wefts move in opposite directions and, because of the nature of the design and technique, they leave slits in the weave. In a small piece such as this, these will not show in the completed tapestry, especially when care is taken to keep the small selvedges regular and even. If any should show, simply sew them together afterwards. Note the outside warp thread which is used as a guideline*

together lengthways, leave the ends long for fringing. Cut a sample out fairly roughly if it is only for future reference, but if it is sufficiently interesting for display as a wall hanging, sew the top ends into the weave but fringe the lower edge. Decide first; cut later.

There are minor variations of the interlocking techniques—single and double—which could be explored. The result is a loss of hard edge definition between one area of weft and another, but you will be able to experiment with curves, free form shapes and pictorial themes.

If you are working blind, that is with no preconceived idea for a design but allowing one shape or colour to stimulate the next, then begin with only two colours for maximum impact. Wind the strips of rag into small manageable balls, or wind them into figure of eight bows, whichever is the easier to carry through the warp.

Using one colour, leave a long end for sewing or pushing into the fabric on completion, then weave in and out as follows:
Pick 1: *Work under one end, then over the next. *Repeat from * to * across the warp.
Pick 2: * Work over one end, then under the next. * Repeat from * to * across the warp.

These two picks are the basis of plainweave. The term 'pick' applies to each single passage of the weft through the warp.

When you need to join in a new length of weft, either start at the edge in the same way as when you begin to weave, or overlap the old and new weft by about 5cm (2in). If the ends should protrude from the finished tapestry, you can either sew them in or push them into the weave with the blunt end of a curved needle.

If you have an idea for a design, approach it in one of two ways: either begin working along the lines visualized but allow for the possibility of the initial idea developing or even altering completely as the pattern builds up, or consider drafting an accurate pattern, known as 'cartoon'. This means working out your design to the right size on a piece of paper, and then taping or hanging it behind the frame so that you can see the pattern through the warp. Then simply weave it as you see it, section by section.

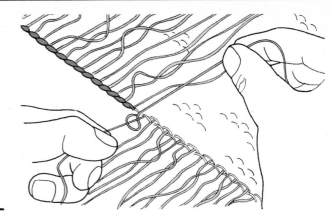

Once a piece is finished and released from the frame, the warp ends should be finished off. There are various ways to do this to decorative effect. For a firm straight edge, take the second warp thread from the left-hand side in your left hand. With the first thread in your right hand, take it over and under the second as illustrated. Take the second over and under the third and so on across the warp.

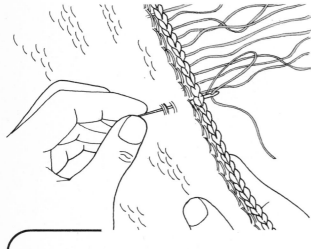

Work a second row in the opposite direction in reverse and then sew each end back into the woven fabric with a large curved needle. John Hinchcliffe often works four rows of knots for a strong and attractive finish. Trim off the excess neatly and tuck any length still showing between the rags.

Fringing is attractive and can be worked in any number of patterns. The simplest is knotted. Take two pairs of warp ends and knot them all together close to the edge. Work across until all the threads are knotted and then trim if necessary.

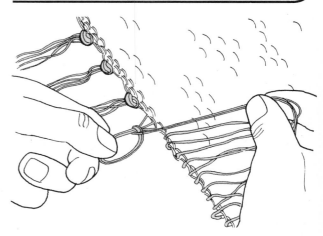

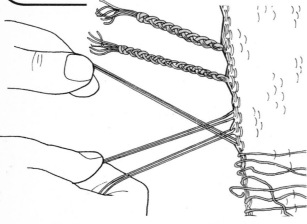

A rather more decorative alternative is to plait or braid the ends. Plait three pairs of warp ends together, then knot at the bottom. Trim as required. A soft, loosely spun warp will fray slightly and look better if uneven; a firmer, closely spun warp looks better if trimmed to an equal length.

Tapestry also lends itself to the incorporation of various types of materials. As well as rags of various types, weights and textures, try using yarns with matt or shiny finishes, fashion yarns such as poodle and mohair, raffia, string and virtually anything which is sufficiently strong and pliable for the work. You can also introduce beads or natural objects such as pierced stones, shells, nuts and bark. With such freedom of expression you can easily produce three-dimensional designs on either geometric or figurative themes. Perhaps the materials that you choose will give you an idea for the theme of the tapestry. For example, a visit to the seaside could yield both materials and inspiration.

*Above: Dyed cotton rags in four different colours have been incorporated into this interesting tapestry. The bottom half has the diagonal stripes moving to the left, and this direction is then reversed in the top portion. This design would prove dynamic if repeated on long strips sewn together. The overall effect would be of a pattern zigzagging over the entire surface of the completed rug. The ends have been strengthened prior to being sewn into the fabric*

# Project 5: Weaving on a Table Loom

John Hinchcliffe shows you, step-by-step, how to make a warp and dress the loom ready for work. Then, having explained how to read and work out weave patterns, he demonstrates the versatility of plainweave and 2/2 twill in flat rag rug making

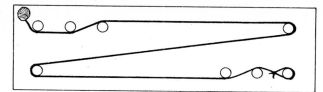

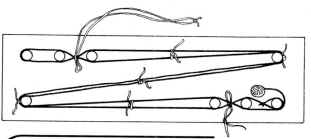

To set up the warp on your table loom, begin winding your warp thread onto a three metre warping board. Tie the free end securely around the bottom left peg, then wind in and out of the next two pegs, take it right across the board to the single peg directly opposite and then diagonally across the board to the other peg top right. Move across to the trio of pegs top left and wind in, out and around. This is your first warp end, length three metres. Repeat 44 times for 44 ends.

To make counting as easy and accurate as possible, tie a loop of thread through each group of ten ends at one of the points where ties are indicated. You will also need to make long ties at the two important raddle crosses to secure the threads and keep them all together. Tie the crosses where marked and make ties at both ends and on each group of threads in the centre of the board. There should be seven ties in all.

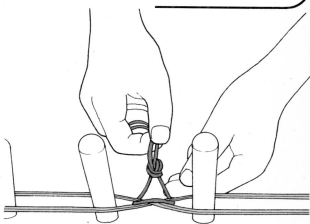

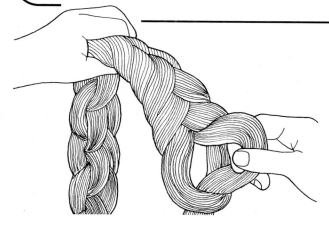

To keep the warp under control and prevent the threads tangling when it is transferred to the loom, create a chain. Lift the warp from a peg away from one of the raddle crosses, leaving the main part still on the board. Position the warp across your wrist, then pull it through the loop so formed. Slip your hand through the new loop and grasp the warp again. Repeat until all the warp is chained.

*Left: This four-shaft table loom is dressed and ready for action. Some models, such as the loom illustrated, depend on the shaft being lifted and lowered by means of strings on the top rather than levers at the side*

You will need a four-shaft table loom. This is shown in detail on page 36 so turn back and familiarize yourself with its various parts and their functions. The diagrammatic reference above the loom will help you understand the step-by-step instructions for dressing the loom that follow over the next few pages.

Basic equipment is shown and explained in detail on pages 38 and 39, so refer back if you need to. Cut and prepare your rags ready for weaving.

Working on a table loom is probably the most practical and direct way of designing for woven rag rugs. It allows you the freedom to experiment. You can produce strips for sewing together and

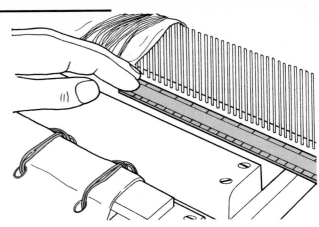

With the warp thus prepared, move to the back of the table loom. Measure out the width of the warp onto the raddle with a ruler and pencil in preparation for spacing it out correctly with the right number of ends to the inch or equivalent in centimetres.

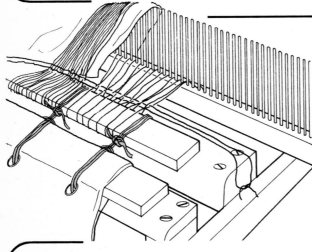

Place the back stick of the back beam through the crossed end of the chained warp. Tie the stick to the apron of the back beam as shown. The raddle cross in the warp makes it easy for you to pick out the threads in their correct order ready for threading them through the raddle.

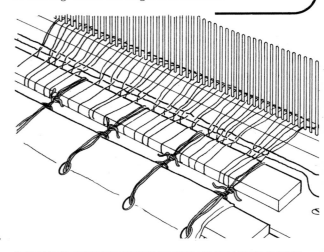

Space out the threads along the back stick and thread them through the raddle to the correct measured width of the warp. The raddle cross is clearly visible interlaced through the ends and lying as a long loop. Once this is done you are ready to wind the warp onto the back beam.

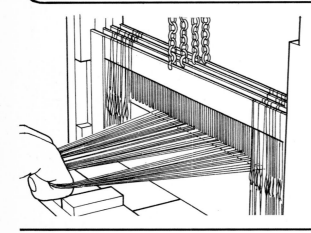

It will help in the next stage to have someone to help you: one person holding the warp under even tension at the front of the loom, the other turning the back beam at the back of the loom to roll on the warp. At the front, comb the warp with your fingers in smallish groups, adjusting them as necessary until all are evenly tensioned. Make sure there are no loose or uneven ends, then pull evenly on them altogether as illustrated.

try out new ideas, operating the shafts by hand. And once you understand how to design, you will be able to weave larger and more ambitious pieces and samples on stronger, more stable foot-operated floor looms.

Most of the techniques for producing rag rugs can be tested on the four-shaft loom, and this includes the tapestry techniques you learned and put into practice in the previous project. However, John Hinchcliffe specializes in making rugs in which the weft crosses the entire width of the warp rather than concentrating the weave into small areas, so this project emphasizes the techniques this involves.

Just as there are techniques allied specifically to working by hand, there are those that rely on the way in which the shafts are threaded and the order in which they are raised and lowered to produce certain structures of weave—twills, double weave and corduroys, for instance.

However before you begin to explore these possibilities, you must begin at the very beginning and set up your loom ready for work and in preparation for the weaving process itself. This setting up is known as 'dressing' the loom. So look at all the parts and understand their function before you begin.

Of prime importance are the shafts, which we shall label 1, 2, 3 and 4, from front to back. The picture on page 68 shows the warp running from the back beam through the various parts, to the cloth beam at the front, onto which your woven fabric will be rolled on completion. Dressing the loom involves this threading up of the warp, so choosing a warp yarn is your first consideration. John Hinchcliffe prefers a linen thread, but hemp, though coarser, is cheaper. The great advantage of linen is that it is very strong and smooth, so for rug warps, select threads described as 6/10 or 4/8.

Next, decide how many warp ends to the inch or equivalent in centimetres you require for the piece you intend weaving. Not only must you decide on the width, but the length too, so that you can estimate how long your warp should be.

When considering the number of ends to the set measurement, decide on the character and

*Below: This detail is from a very large rug of Indian origin, worked entirely in plain-weave. It has been woven in a completely unplanned way with a random selection of rags, all in cotton*

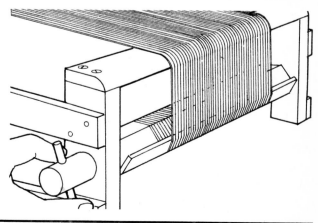

*Once the warp is prepared at the front of the loom and is being held in readiness, begin winding it onto the back beam at the back of the loom. As the beam turns, insert sticks or pieces of brown paper to prevent the ends building up on top of one another and perhaps tangling.*

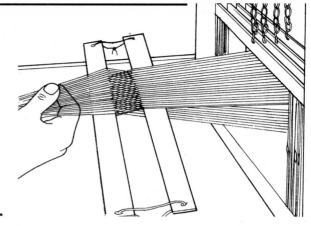

*When the end cross is within 8cm (3in) of the shafts, the warp being fully wound onto the back beam, remove the raddle and insert cross sticks to replace the tie made initially on the warping board or mill. Tie the cross sticks together to keep them parallel to one another and to prevent them falling out of the warp. Cut the tie and remove the string.*

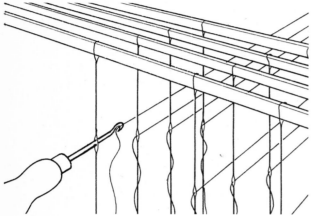

*Push the cross sticks through so that they and the cross are at the back behind the healds, then cut across the warp ends and tie them in small groups ready for threading through the healds. Thread the ends through in the correct order with the aid of a threading hook. Once each group has been pulled through, re-tie to stop them slipping back through the eyes in the healds.*

*Release the back warp roller and pull the warp forward by about 25 to 30cm (10 to 12in) through the cross sticks and the healds. Position yourself in the centre of the loom, place the reed in the batten and find the exact centre of the reed with a ruler and pencil. Measure out each side to the correct width of warp just as you did on the raddle. Then begin to draw the ends through the dents in the reed with the reed hook.*

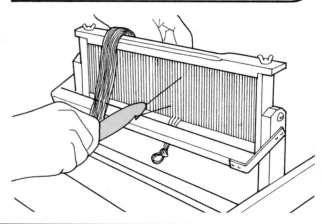

nature of your intended rug. How thick is it to be? What rags will you be using? In most plain and twill weave rugs, the weft usually hides the warp completely, but to do this satisfactorily you must establish early on in the proceedings the correct and balanced relationship between warp and weft.

When John Hinchcliffe weaves a rag rug, he uses a 6/10 linen thread for the warp and a 2/55 carpet wool and rags for the weft. For a heavy warp—3 ends per 2.5cm (1in)—he uses the warp singly or doubly with a 4 or 6 plied weft. More ordinarily, with 4 ends per 2.5cm (1in), he plies 3 or 4 weft threads together. Generally speaking, the greater the number of warp ends per 2.5cm

(1in), the finer the weft should be. Following this through, a thinnish rag rug might have 6 ends per 2.5cm (1in) with a weft of 2/55 rug wool used singly and strips of rag.

For the novice rug weaver, however, John Hinchcliffe suggests that because weaving with cloth strips is more difficult than weaving with a wool weft, and as a result you may find it initially difficult to cover the warp ends satisfactorily, you should use a setting of 3 ends per 2.5cm (1in) and experiment with various types of fabric.

When determining the correct warp setting, allow a few extra ends for working the sides or the 'selvedges'. These will strengthen them considerably. So, having decided on the number of warp ends per 2.5cm (1in), decide how wide you want your piece to be. Hopefully, you will be working on a fairly narrow table loom as anything too wide will lack sufficient strength for weaving samples and strips in quantity. The twill samples on pages 78/79 are all 30.5cm (12in) wide which is the widest you should attempt.

To estimate the number of warp ends required, look at a particular situation. Imagine that you have decided upon a warp setting of 4 ends per 2.5cm (1in) and a width of 25cm (10in).

All you have to do is multiply the two figures for the total number of warp ends required, in this case 40. Add two on each side for the selvedges and you have a total of 44 ends in all.

The last factor for consideration is the length of the warp. This could be determined by the length of the piece to be woven or the number of samples you envisage weaving. You must take into account any waste between one sample and another, and how you want to finish the ends once the piece or pieces have been cut from the loom. For a collection of samples 25cm (10in) square, a three metre warping board for a three metre warp should be quite sufficient.

Plainweave is the simplest of all the weave patterns and can be described very easily in words. Once you begin trying some of the more complex weaves however, it is easier to show them in draft form. On most weave plans, a mark in a square indicates that at this particular inter-

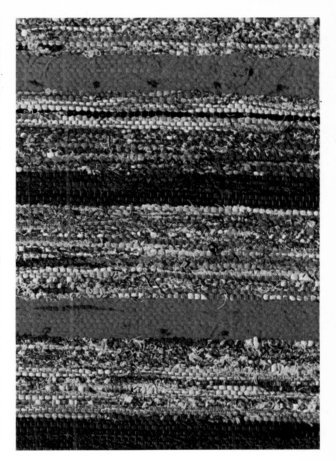

## Weave notation

 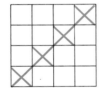 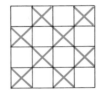

## A full analysis of the weave

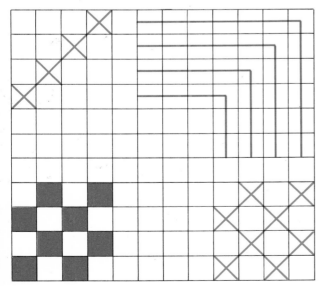

*Above: Detail from a flat Greek rag rug in which the warp shows as much as the weft. Two colours have been dyed to provide regular stripes in a pre-arranged pattern, while the areas in between are filled in a random manner*

*Left: There are three forms of weave notation: the weave diagram shown at the left, the draft for threading the loom, in the centre, and a lifting plan for the shafts, shown on the right. These three pieces of information are usually placed together to give a full analysis of the weave. Though you may come across them in varying forms in different books, they all give this basic information in one way or another. Weaves are also often shown diagrammatically from the side, each circle representing an end and the weft drawn as a line running under and over the ends in the correct order*

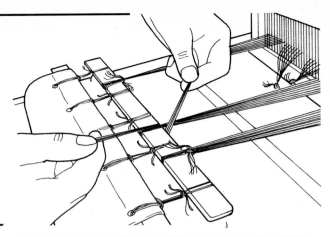

*If your warp is set to 4 ends per 2.5cm (1in) and the reed is 4 dents per 2.5cm (1in), thread one end through each dent. At the selvedges, thread them double as you did through the healds. As you pull through each group of ends, tie them together to stop them slipping back. Once they are all threaded through, tie the outside groups to the front beam stick under tension. Then tie the other groups, working into the centre.*

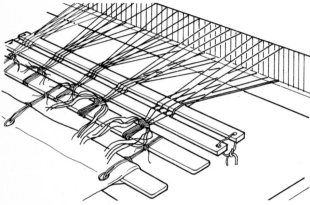

*To pull tight and tension properly, place the flat of your hand over the warp, adjusting any ends that try to slip back, and tie to the beam stick with a reef knot. Tighten the warp beam and secure the ratchet. Lift shafts 1 and 3 and place a stick into the resulting shed. Lower the shafts. Lift shafts 2 and 4 and insert a second stick into this new shed. Push the sticks towards the warp beam. You now have a firm base to begin weaving against.*

section the warp end is on the surface or the face of the fabric and the pick underneath. It is normal to use a filled in square to show an end over a pick, and a blank square to show a pick over an end.

The most straightforward draft or threading order of the warp ends through the healds is known as a straight draft. And it is from this that the 2/2 twills are derived, as is plainweave, but the latter can be worked with only two shafts whereas twills require four.

Floor looms with pedals require a pedal tie-up-plan and a pre-determined pedalling order. Table looms, however, require a lifting plan for the shafts which are raised and lowered from fixed positions.

Although any weaving plan is usually put down onto squared paper, it is important to note that in weaving—and rag weaving in particular, where the weft usually hides the warp—the weave plan gives very little idea of the appearance of the woven fabric of the rug, but it is intended to indicate, in the clearest possible way, the interlacing of warp and weft. On all plans, the vertical rows equal the warp ends, the horizontal rows the weft picks.

Plainweave, or 'tabby', may appear limiting but the opposite is in fact true. It is the most useful of all the techniques for creative work, for not only can you work it with only two shafts, but it is the basis of many allied techniques. The beginner

would be well advised to study many of the possibilities of plainweave and then create a sampler to put them into practice. This will enable you to grasp the differences between normal weaving, plainweaving which covers the warp, and the techniques that result from manipulating the weft or numerous wefts to form a design, all of which can be based on plainweave.

On its own, plainweave has infinite design possibilities, especially when strips of rag are introduced into the warp. Even in very simple samples, the different patterns and colours in the cloth will produce interesting results. And although a random use of strips is very satisfying, you will soon be tempted to organize the areas of colour, working strips in dyed and undyed fabrics.

As one sample gives you an idea for another, think about plying two strips in different colours or patterns together, or one quality with another. You can also twist two strips for 'S' or 'Z' twist stripes. Alternatively, by using two shuttles carrying two different colours and passing them from selvedge to selvedge alternately, you can achieve weft- and warp-way stripes. And spots are quite easy to achieve too.

Many of the related plainweave techniques differ to plainweave proper in that instead of the weft running from selvedge to selvedge, it covers small areas within the area of the warp. Perhaps the easiest and best known of these is Kelim (see pages 62/63).

Rolaken is a technique commonly attributed to the Scandinavians. It was developed to overcome the problem of the slits left in the woven fabric as a result of using the Kelim method. Basically the weft of the two separate colours being used are interlocked so that they do not leave a slit. The shuttles carrying the two colours work towards one another and are interlocked before they return. Norwegian Rolaken always interlocks the wefts in the same direction in order to keep the work flat. That is the wefts are carried towards one another, they meet between two warp threads, they loop and return. On the reverse row, the threads do not cross, this results in a clear and definite join which means in effect, that the rug is reversible.

The so-called Swedish method is very much the same. The first row of the weft moves to the right, but the interlocking is repeated on the return journey. Each weft comes up from underneath the one which crosses it and up to the right before returning to the left from whence it came. This technique does not result in a reversible rug. Though the joins will be clear and definite on the face of the rug, there will be distinct ridges on the underside.

*Right: Detail of a Swedish floral rug which is woven in plainweave. The motifs have been introduced by the simple but effective means of inlaying*

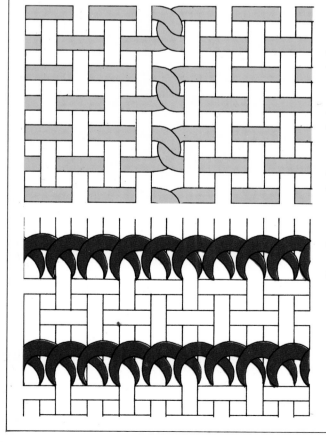

*These drawings illustrate the techniques associated with plainweave for flat rugs. Top left: Norwegian Rolaken, top right: inlaying, bottom left: Soumack*

*You may find that the warp threads are not lying parallel to one another. This is because they have been tied to the front cloth beam in groups. Correct by winding 6 or 7 thicknesses of warp yarn onto a shuttle and then work a few centimetres of plainweave. This 'fat' weft will space the ends and tension them evenly.*

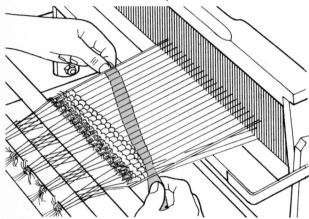

*Once your warp ends are correctly spaced and are lying parallel to one another, you can begin to weave with strips of rag, prepared and cut to width. To keep the edges straight so that the piece is of even width, you must lay in each strip at an angle to allow for ease when beating down. Work simple plainweave, inserting the rag into the shed either wound into a small ball or onto a flat shuttle.*

*As each pick is inserted, pull the reed in the batten towards you firmly to beat the rag against the woven fabric. The two sticks will give you a solid base to beat down upon. Beat down so that as little warp shows as possible, or if you want the particular effect—where the warp shows as much as the weft, apply less pressure.*

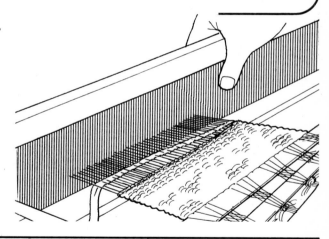

Some of the best plainweave techniques, however, that John Hinchcliffe feels are especially related to rag rugs and the making of bedspreads, are those that use an inlay to produce a motif or pattern (see page 75). The inlay is simply extra weft laid into the plainweave. Many Scandinavian and Canadian bedspreads use this technique with often exceptionally beautiful results. It can be, and often is, of any material—wool, rag or fleece, for instance.

There are many variations of the inlaying technique, inlay simply meaning at its most basic the insertion or 'laying in' of a different material to the one being used for the plainweave. Spots of colour can be introduced very easily and many beautiful effects can be achieved by simply laying in long strips to reproduce simple pile effects. Obviously there is a great deal of scope here for the weaver.

The last group of techniques related to plainweave are those worked by hand. Though plainweave is the basis of the structure, the actual form or design is manipulated dextrously.

Soumack means' weft wrapping and the technique has similarities to a part of tapestry weaving Soumack resembles a knitted garter stitch in appearance (see page 75) but has a concealed plainweave weft beneath the surface. It can be used in a variety of ways—with plainweave worked on alternate rows, for instance. Also note that in some variations of Soumack the weft does not wrap around only one warp end at a time, but as many as you choose. Likewise, you are not restricted to just one row of Soumack, but as many as you want.

Apart from the techniques for creating flat rag rugs based on plainweave, there exist a range of other possibilities. These utilize the infinite variations of threading the warp through the healds on the shafts, and then the sequence of raising and lowering them. In most of these loom techniques, the weft is generally passed from one selvedge to another which greatly speeds the process of weaving. But although in one respect this limits the design potential, it creates other possibilities.

To introduce these shaft controlled methods,

*Below: This exceptionally finely woven American sheet or thin blanket shows the tartan or plaid effect that is the conclusion of dressing the loom with a multicoloured striped warp and then working plainweave, also in stripes. It is worked in cotton rags throughout*

# Project 5

John Hinchcliffe has used a straight four-shaft draft which is the very simplest and most straightforward way to thread the shafts and the classic 2/2 twill as an example of a simple weave that relies on the way the warp is threaded. The term 2/2—the two numbers separated by a diagonal line—can be explained very simply. The first number refers to the number of ends each weft pick passes under in one repeat of the twill, while the second refers to the number of ends it passes over. The 2/2 twill is possibly the most widely used twill in weaving, and especially rug weaving, where it offers many colour and weave effects as a weft faced structure, and an excellent strong construction for rugs.

This type of twill differs to the normal twill as used in the construction of cloth where the warp and weft are visible, producing the characteristic twill lines running diagonally across the fabric. In the 2/2 structure, the warp is completely hidden, but if a weft of a single colour is used, fine ridges will appear running with the twill. However, the technique becomes increasingly more interesting as more coloured wefts are used and the sequences in which they are used are changed.

After experimenting with the straight 2/2 twill, try the broken version which has the same lifting sequence but where the order of the last two is reversed. For example: 1+2/ 2+3/ 4+1/ 3+4. This effectively breaks the straight twill sequence, cancelling out the resulting twill ridges or lines.

Alternatively try combining different colour and pick sequences, by moving from a straight 2/2 twill sequence into a broken 2/2 twill sequence or by varying the colours and materials in use.

The last 2/2 twill that John Hinchcliffe feels is worth careful consideration is a construction known as 2/2 twill woven on opposites. This gives interesting results and a clearly defined design plus the bonus of a strong structure for rug making.

In this weave, the lifting of the shafts is based on the normal straight 2/2 twill sequence of 1+2, 2+3, 3+4 and 4+1. However, after every one of these normal picks, it's opposite is lifted. For example, the opposite of 1+2 is 3+4, the opposite of 2+3 is 1+4, the opposite of 3+4 is 1+2 and the opposite of 4+1 is 2+3.

If the normal pick is in one colour and the opposite pick in another (this is if two colours are used throughout), then clearly defined oblique lines will appear in these two colours. And a very good zigzag twill will be the result of reversing the colour sequence after each lifting repeat.

To ensure that you make a really good firm edge with all twill fabrics, a floating selvedge is recommended. To work this, leave the outside warp on each side unthreaded. In other words do not thread them through the healds, so that they remain in a constant position and will not move with the remainder of the warp. Then as you pass the weft from one side to the other, take it under or over the floating ends to lock the weft.

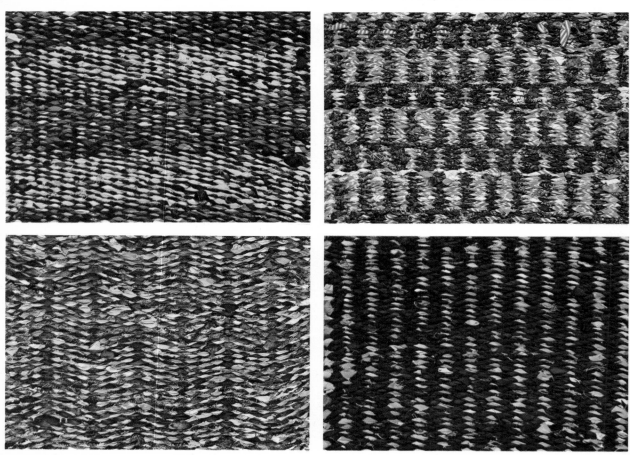

All the samples of 2/2 twill shown on these two pages have been woven with a warp setting of 4 ends per 2.5cm (1in) with double ends at the selvedges for additional strength at these potentially weak points. In a mixture of dyed and undyed cotton rags, they are all based on the ordinary straightforward repeat and consist mainly of two differently coloured wefts used in various sequences. The drawing above shows the notation for a normal 2/2 twill sequence

# Project 6: Weaving in Strips

John Hinchcliffe introduces some of the pile techniques associated with plainweave and then concentrates on the potential of strip weaving. Not only is this very practical, but careful planning enables the weaver to design sophisticated rugs and bedspreads, carpets and coverlets

In many primitive societies strip weaving was the norm rather than the exception. As looms had to be narrow for ease of carriage for the nomadic tribes, and wide looms made of natural materials locally to hand were often not strong or stable enough to weave anything very wide, craftsmen and women developed the art of creating narrow pieces that could be sewn together for larger pieces. Examples of strip weaving can be traced back to the very earliest times.

There are two main factors for consideration in weaving a large piece of work from smaller strips. The first is that no weaver really has a loom that is big enough to weave the largest rug that he or she may want to weave, even with the quite large looms that are available today. So even with the narrowest of table looms, the technique offers a great deal of scope.

The second valuable aspect of weaving in strips is that it opens up an enormous range of design possibilities as illustrated by the Ashanti strip rug on this page. There are other advantages too, depending on the techniques employed. For instance, in plainweaving, where the weft passes from selvedge to selvedge in an uninterrupted manner, you can weave a strip very quickly. Alternatively, should you choose to interrupt the passage of the weft with blocks of colour requiring three separate wefts for three distinct and separate colour blocks, then the work will be slowed down considerably. Should you pursue this approach, you will probably use plainweaving in conjunction with Kelim, or the Rolaken technique of interlocking the separate areas in conjunction with one another. However, by weaving three separate strips you will gain a great deal of time. being able to work right across the weft and working each strip in the colour of your choice.

And once you begin to weave stripes or blocks of colour, design possibilities begin to occur almost immediately. Such areas could be staggered or you could build up diagonals of colour or pattern. Not only do many African blankets explore such ideas but many old Scandinavian Rya rugs exhibit a defiance of the apparent limitations of the technique. These are often in two halves, being made up of two or more pieces.

There are several factors that you should consider before and during weaving strips which are to be sewn together. Firstly, you must constantly check that your warp is evenly tensioned and that the selvedges remain quite parallel to one another. When you come to sew the pieces up, if the edges go inwards or outwards, you will either have gaps in the seams or the rug will buckle. Also, remember to measure and mark the strips whilst you weave them to make sure they are all the same length, and that any colour changes or stripes will match up once the strips are assembled. When John Hinchcliffe is working strips for one of his rugs, he inserts a piece of wool every 15cm (6in) or so to keep a check on his progress.

*Left: This fine piece of African weaving by the Ashanti tribe from one of the regions of Ghana is in vividly coloured pure silk. The weaver has carefully preplanned the design and then worked each strip individually ready for sewing together. This was made necessary because of the small looms which the tribes used. This cloth was worn by the chiefs on ceremonial occasions*

Before progressing to details of how strips should be assembled, consider some of the alternative methods of adding interest to your woven rugs. Though the Swedes developed a liking for insertions (inlays)—either single pieces of fabric to resemble bows in the fabric, or in blocks to create simple or complex patterns—there are various pile techniques based on plainweave that are valuable in rag rug making.

Before progressing to the traditional pile techniques—Rya, Turkish and Persian hand knotting—consider a very simple way to create a pile effect. All you have to do is pull up a loop of the weft at regular intervals, either across the width of the warp or in small areas to produce a contrast of texture. The resulting loops can either be left as they are or cut. Try working rows of plainweave between them or mass or scatter them completely at random.

Rags can be knotted into the warp ends in rows across the width of the warp and secured by alternate rows of plainweave. The two traditional methods are the Turkish and the Giordes form of knotting (see page 85). The term 'Rya'—Rya rugs being native to Finland—describes an approach rather than a method. Rows of hand knotting are interspersed with quite wide areas of plainweave, thus allowing the pile to lie down rather than stand upright. Rya rugs were originally woven as bedcovers as well as floor rugs, and their history is long and interesting.

*Above: Strips of rag weaving have long been a feature of home furnishing in Swedish homes. The room above shows long lengths of rag weave used as rugs, while in the centre, the table stands on two pieces joined to make a large square rug. These rugs were constantly moved to prevent wear*

*Right: This coverlet is typical of those created in all good Swedish homes for hundreds of years. Interest has been added to this cotton rag rug in the form of colourful rag insertions*

The Turkish knot is used in Rya rugs and again they are held in place in the woven fabric with rows or areas of plainweave. The pile can be as short or as long as you like. There is no need to be bound by tradition. The rules are there to be broken in the pursuit of creative satisfaction.

As in all knotting techniques, the pile can be very rich and in a combination of fabrics and yarns. By varying these and the spacing between the areas of knots, you can produce rugs and bedspreads of quite different qualities.

The main thing to remember when working with the Rya technique is to decide exactly what quality you want to reproduce. If you prefer an all over long pile, experiment on a small sample piece to find out how many rows of plainweave between each row of knotting is required. Alternatively,

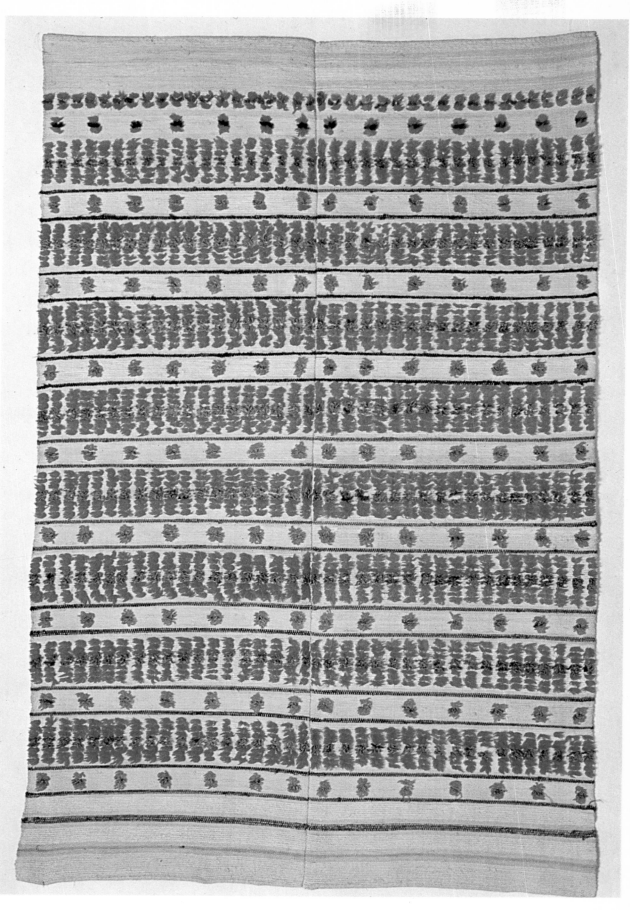

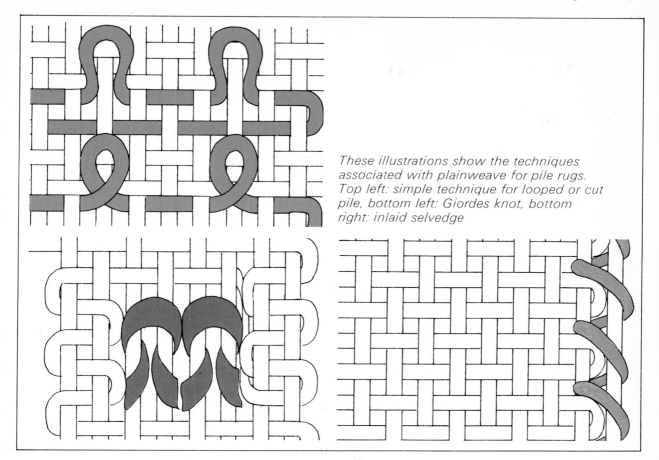

*These illustrations show the techniques associated with plainweave for pile rugs. Top left: simple technique for looped or cut pile, bottom left: Giordes knot, bottom right: inlaid selvedge*

*Left: John Hinchcliffe creates many of his beautiful rugs from strips, using either hand knotted pile in conjunction with plainweave, or by laying in strips, the loops of which are cut afterwards, a technique that is very much his own. Although this rug has been worked at random, the fact that he uses the same range of colours throughout holds the overall design together*

you may want bands of pile with areas of plain-weave in rags or wool showing inbetween. You can either knot the pile from fairly uneven lengths of cut yarn or rag for a very shaggy effect, work with long continuous strips, or cut over a guide bar for a more regular pile.

There are other uses for hand knotting characterized by a short pile. By working smaller areas of plainweave between the knots, the pile is forced into an upright position. Eastern rugs use this approach extensively. Cut the pile every few rows and bang the underside of the rug to make the pile stand up. This will enable you to trim the pile to even length.

When working a knotted rug, or a rug that is partially knotted for decoration, note that the selvedges at the sides should not bear any knots. The edges of any rug are vulnerable, so use them to protect the areas of knots within the rug. They can also be strengthened by either working in an extra weft, or the more common method of weaving extra picks of plainweave to compensate for the absence of knots along the edge (above).

Note that the closer the warp is set, the closer the knots will lie in the horizontal position and the more intricate the design can therefore be. Close examination of some fine Eastern rugs would prove this to be so—especially those woven in silk. However, it is more usual today to use relatively coarse settings, especially where the emphasis is on exploring particular colour and textural effects, using either cloth or wool on their own or in combination.

In some countries, Sweden in particular, there is an interest in working areas of plainweave and pile so that the knotted sections stand out in relief against a flat background. This too opens a great many design possibilities.

Joining the strips together is a relatively simple matter. Place them flat on the floor, checking first of all that you have them in the correct order according to your pre-planned design. Then make sure that the initial picks of the plainweave are in the correct position. If not, it may be necessary to unpick a few rows from whichever end of the strip is not lying true and where you intend to start sewing. Note that it is important to start sewing at one end, and one end only.

Fringe all the strips at one end. Then begin sewing the strips together starting from the fringed ends and stopping when you reach the unfringed ends. You may find that you have to

*Above: In this pile rug, John Hinchcliffe has developed the design possibilities in strip weaving. He has achieved a staggered effect by planning the design of the strips and the overall results beforehand*

*Right: To sew the strips of rag together in the first method, sew up and over between the end of the warp threads of each strip, pulling firmly but not too tightly so that the edges butt up against each other. Alternatively, you may prefer the second method below. Simply sew down through the fabric of the weave along the edge of each strip as indicated*

unpick a little of the weave if the strips are out of line here too.

Use a strong curved carpet or upholstery needle or a blunt tapestry needle and thread it with the same thread as used in the weaving of the strips themselves. There are two effective ways to sew the strips together and these are illustrated below. It might be worthwhile, however, to see whether you can develop an even more reliable method yourself.

Try not to be tempted to sew strips together that have been woven at different times. A strip that has been lying around for a month or more will have settled, and its tension altered. A new strip cut direct from the loom will be tighter and less flexible. As a result, the sewing of the two together will not be at all satisfactory. In sewing his pile rugs together, John Hinchcliffe works from the back.

If strip weaving is a fairly new concept for you, it would be well worth looking around at further examples for ideas and stimulation. Specialist books, .museums and private collections will provide background material for your experiments and inspiration for your designs. In most cases, you will be amazed at the versatility of the technique, soon recognizing that the restrictions of quite a small loom need in no way affect your creativity. You need not be afraid that, after purchasing your loom it will then remain unused because the possibilities are endless and exciting.

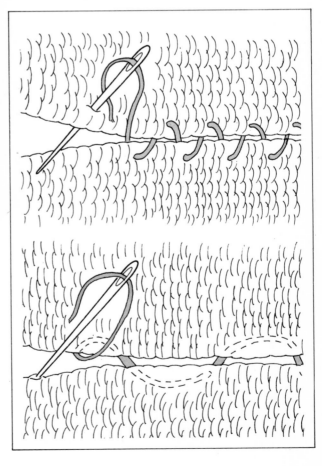

*Below: A flat coverlet but in plainweave—here the staggering is in alternate rows of dyed and undyed rags for a very different effect altogether. The plan to which John Hinchcliffe worked for the coverlet below is shown on the right. He drew out the number of squares for the blocks of colour, and then taped a small piece of the fabric he intended to use in each. In this way, he was able to plan the individual strips, but of course, once woven, all the fabrics changed in tone and quality*

# Project 7: Weaving on a Floor Loom

In the final project, John Hinchcliffe introduces you to the loom on which he weaves large rugs. He identifies the various parts, describes the shedding mechanism and offers some general hints and tips on weaving with rags

One of the main requirements of any loom is that it should be strong, and this applies throughout the range of table and floor looms. This is as necessary when weaving narrow strips as it is when working a piece under a very high warp tension and requiring a very firm and heavy beating down of the weft. It is not surprising therefore that many of the frames used in the rug and carpet industry are of metal rather than wood.

Obviously, the type of frame you require depends very much on the type of rug you want to weave, how intensive your production is to be and how serious you are about the craft. A large floor loom is neither a cheap nor simple affair, but it does have the advantage of allowing a large number of pieces to be worked, and even wider strips for wider rugs and rag carpets.

Since the acquisition of a large loom is not a matter to be treated lightly, certain factors should be taken into consideration. A loom is a tool, and as with most tools there are those that are cheaper and of inferior quality, and those that are more expensive, but worth every penny in terms of reliability and quality. The loom shown on page 37 displays some excellent features. The main parts are in a good hard wood giving strength where necessary and it is particularly good for weaving rugs. It is Danish, but there are Swedish looms that are of equal quality. In Scandinavia, the horizontal frame loom has long become acceptable for weaving flat and pile rugs, and it is for this

*Left: John Hinchcliffe at work on his loom. Here he is cutting the loops created by laying in strips of rag. The shuttle, carrying the wool with which he works alternate rows of plainweave to hold the rags firmly in position, can be clearly seen*

*Right: The two types of double counter-march loom showing the various parts and the way in which they are tied up. When pressure (by means of the foot) is applied to the treadles, certain shafts are lowered and the remainder raised, thus making a shed. The method of knotting at the bottom (a simple slip knot) is of great importance as it can be easily adjusted. The tying-up process requires a great deal of adjusting because by this method, the cords may be shortened or lengthened. The knot will not give way no matter what the weight of the pull*

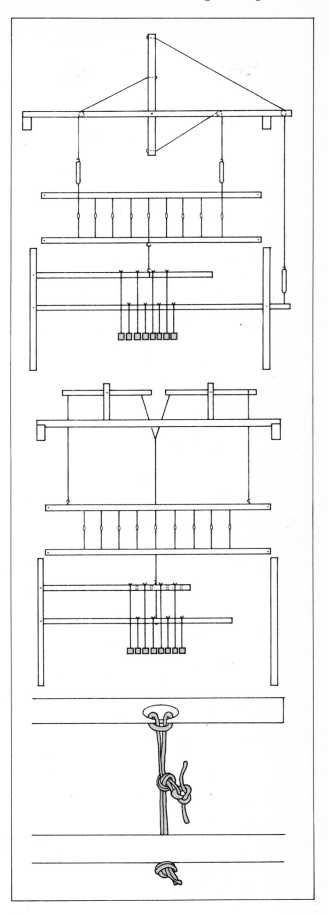

reason that their frames have developed to a high level of excellence and quality and are much sought after all over the world.

Should you have purchased or be about to start work on a large floor loom, there are certain factors that require attention and careful consideration.

**The loom frame.** This should be particularly strong and especially so in the warp and cloth beams and the breast and back beams. On the loom pictured on page 37, these parts are in beech while the rest of the frame is in pine.

**Warp tension.** Because the tension of the warp will be high and under great strain, there will be a lot of strain on the ratchets attached to the front and back beams. It is important, therefore, to check that the ratchets are quite secure and an integral feature of the beams.

**The batten.** The most suitable batten for weaving large rugs is one that is underslung from the top of the loom. And because the batten is responsible for beating and compacting the weft correctly, it should be weighted with a bar of heavy metal or wood. The loom should also be secured to the floor as the beating down of the weft often results in the loom moving across the surface of the floor.

**The pedals.** Choose a loom where the pedals pivot at the back rather than the front. You will find this enables you to open the highly tensioned and wider warp more easily as it is a process that requires quite a lot of force.

**Apron front and back sticks.** The apron on both the warp beam and the cloth beam should be of a strong canvas. The front and back sticks should preferably be metal rather than wood as the pressure exerted upon them may otherwise break or bend them.

**Seat.** A bench seat, or one that is attached to the loom and so an integral part of its design, is essential. Not only must it be comfortable but you will find it useful for spreading out equipment during work.

In project 5, you learned that on a table loom the shafts are simply raised and lowered by means of levers at the side of the loom. This was perfectly adequate for weaving narrow strips where the warp was not under a great deal of strain. In rug weaving, however, where a highly tensioned and often quite inelastic warp is being used, it is easier to obtain a good clear and wide shed through which the shuttle can be passed at speed with a system that not only raises some shafts, but lowers others at the same time. Such a system is called 'double countermarch'.

There are other systems on foot looms, but John Hinchcliffe prefers the double countermarch and recommends it to anyone considering weaving large pieces seriously. It is sufficient to say that these other types of loom, especially those with four-shaft shedding motions or ordinary counter-balance looms with only one set of countermarches (lams) and what are called

*John Hinchcliffe uses two methods of producing pile rugs. In the first he hand knots strips of equal width and length into the warp between picks of wool weft which hold them firmly in place. With the strip across two warp ends as shown, pull the rags through to the surface.*

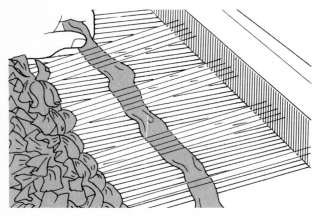

*The second method he uses is based on the technique of weaving corduroy. Strips of rag are inserted into the shed so that long floats lie on the surface. When the weft is beaten down, secure with the necessary number of picks of wool weft. The floats are then cut so that the pile springs to the surface. A large number of shafts are required and this is a complex procedure, so anyone interested in investigating the technique should refer to one of the many specialist books on the subject.*

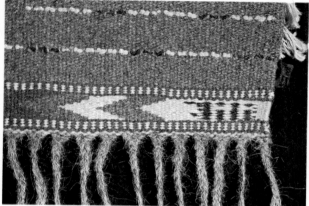

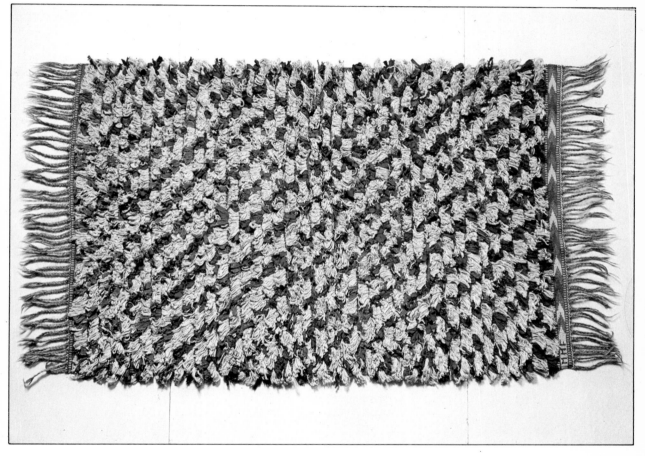

either 'hopeless horses' or 'reliable rollers', rely on a completely balanced movement of the shafts for a good shed. For example, when shaft numbers 1 and 2 are raised, 3 and 4 are automatically lowered. If the design requires, however, that the shafts move in the relation of 1 to 3, then the counter-balance will not be maintained and poor sheds will result.

The double countermarch loom does not work in this way. The shafts do not work in pairs, thus counter-balancing each other, but singly. Each shaft, whatever the number, is attached to two lams and can operate as a single unit. This obviously increases the technical and design possibilities.

*Above: This unusual rug is Swedish and woven this century by Märta Måås of Fjetterström. It incorporates many of the techniques learned through these projects, including plainweave, motifs along the edges, fringing and hand knotting in yarn, hair and rag. It is quite beautifully executed, its overall patterning resembling a twill with its diagonal lines of colour. The details at the top show the weaver's initials worked into the edge of the rug and the same section shown from the reverse side*

*Right: This more recent rug shows John Hinchcliffe's increasing interest in using colour in a vibrant yet harmonious manner*

*Below: An early rug with stripes and lines of zigzag patterning. All the rags are in cotton and have been dyed to the exact colour required*

There are two systems of double counter-march—one has horizontal 'jacks' or 'coupers' supporting the shafts, the other has pulleys and vertical jacks. Both have two sets of lams. Each shaft has an upper lam, the lowering of which lowers the shaft, and a lower lam—usually much longer—which raises the shaft.

Because the shedding motion is positive in its movement up and down, the lams must be tied appropriately with strong thick loom cord. The tying up of the lams can be difficult on a counter-march loom because of the number of ties this entails. Not only will you be tying the shafts you want to be raised, but those to be lowered too.

On a four-shaft loom, four ties are necessary for each pedal. But before tying up, all the parts must be in the fixed horizontal position parallel to one another. On the loom illustrated on page 37, the jacks are pivoted and held by rods inserted to hold the shafts in their correct positions. The lams may need to be adjusted, while a bar at the bottom of the loom holds all the pedals at the same height and at the same angle ready to be tied.

Tie the shafts to be pulled down according to the pattern draft to the pedals from the upper lam. Follow, for example, the pattern for the basic 2/2 twill shown on page 79. In this, the first weft insertion will be where shafts 1 and 2 are lifted. Shafts 3 and 4 will be down. Therefore, the upper lams 3 and 4 are tied to pedal number one, and the lower lams 1 and 2 tied to pedal number two. Therefore four pedals will be required to weave the 2/2 twill, each pedal controlling one of the four different shed movements required by the pattern.

As most looms have more than four pedals, it is usual and in fact advisable to use two more pedals to control the plainweaving at the beginning and end of rugs, especially rag rugs.

The wider the warp on your loom, the more careful you must be to achieve an even tension when placing it on the loom ready for work. The edges too require special attention, so during the weaving or laying in of strips, watch that they remain parallel and the piece does not pull inwards. And the wider the piece is to be, the heavier your beater should be.

If you intend weaving large pieces, you must consider the proportions of the work. John Hinchcliffe's rugs vary in size, but two average sizes he works that seem popular are 90cm×1.5m (3ft×5ft) and 1.8m×1.2m (6ft×4ft). He suggests that to keep a check on your progress, tie a piece of differently coloured rag or yarn every 15—25cm (6—12in). And remember to leave an adequate allowance of warp for finishing.

In a book of this nature it is obviously impossible to give details of all the many aspects associated with the use of large floor looms. We hope however that you will be inspired to investigate the various techniques for yourself and that the ideas in this book have fired your enthusiasm for producing beautiful rag rugs.

# Bibliography

ATWATER, Mary, *Design and the Handweaver,* Shuttle Craft Guild Monographs, HTH Publishers, California 1961

ATWATER, Mary, *Guatemala Visited,* Shuttle Craft Guild Monographs, HTH Publishers, California 1965

BEUTLICH, Tadek, *Technique of Woven Tapestry,* Batsford (B.T.) Ltd., London 1967; Watson-Guptill Publications, New York 1967

BURNHAM, H. B. and D. K., *Keep Me Warm One Night: Early Handweaving in Eastern Canada,* University of Toronto Press 1973

CHETWYND, Hilary, *Simple Weaving,* Studio Vista Publishers, London 1969; Watson-Guptill Publications, New York 1969

COLLINGWOOD, Peter, *Techniques of Rag Weaving,* Faber & Faber Ltd., London 1969; Watson-Guptill Publications, New York 1969

DAVENPORT, Elsie, *Your Handspinning,* Select Books, California 1964

DYER, Anne, *Dyes from Natural Sources,* Branford Publishers, Massachussetts 1976

FELCHER, Cecelia, *The Complete Book of Rug Making,* Hale, London 1975; Hawthorn Books Inc., New York 1975

HALSEY, M. and YOUNGMARK, Lore, *Foundations of Weaving,* David & Charles, Newton Abbot 1975; Watson-Guptill Publications, New York 1975

ITTEN, Johannes, *Elements of Colour,* Van Nostrand Reinhold Co Ltd., New York 1971

KERIMOV, L., *Folk Designs from the Caucasus for Weaving and Needlework,* Dover Publications, New York 1975

KIRBY, Mary, *Designing on the Loom,* The Studio Publications, London and New York 1975; reprinted USA 1973 by Select Books, California

KOPP, Joel and Kate, *American Hooked and Sewn Rugs: Folk Art Underfoot,* Dutton Paperback Original, New York 1975

LEADBEATER, Eliza, *Handspinning,* Studio Vista Publishers, London 1976; Branford Publishers, Massachussetts 1976

MAREIN, Shirley, *Creating Rugs and Wall Hangings,* Studio Vista Publishers, London 1975; Viking Press, New York 1975

STRAUB, Marianne, *Hand Weaving and Cloth Design,* Pelham Books Ltd., London 1977; Viking Press, New York 1977

THURSTAN, Violetta, *Use of Vegetable Dyes for Beginners,* Reeves Dryad Press, Enfield, Middx 1967; reprinted USA 1977 by Basic Crafts, New York

TIDBALL, H., *Color and Dyeing,* Shuttle Craft Guild Monographs, HTH Publishers, California 1965
*The Double Weave,* Shuttle Craft Guild Monographs, HTH Publishers, California 1960
*Peter Collingwood: His Weaves and Weaving,* Shuttle Craft Guild Monographs, HTH Publishers, California 1963
*Weaving Inkle Bands,* Shuttle Craft Guild Monographs, HTH Publishers, California 1969

# Suppliers

## Australasia

Carpet Manufacturers Ltd., 11–27 Harris Road, Five Dock, NSW 2046 (yarns)

Druva Handweaving Pty Ltd., 373–375 Camberwell Road, Camberwell, Victoria 3124 (weaving equipment)

Golding Industries Handicraft Centre, 158 Cuba Street, Wellington, New Zealand (mail order)

Marianne's Craft Shop, 468 Guinea Street, Albury NSW 2640 (Swedish and Australian looms)

Several Arts, 63 Jersey Road, Woollahra, NSW 2025 (rugmaking supplies)

Wondoflex Yarn Craft Centre, 1353 Malvern Road, Malvern Victoria 3144 (yarns and weaving equipment)

## North America

William Condon & Sons Ltd., Charlottetown, Prince Edward Island, Canada. (yarn)

Craft Industries, 1513 and 1516 W. Alabama, Houston, Texas 77006. (natural dyes)

Craft Service, 337 University Avenue, Rochester, N.Y. 14607.

Intertwine, 217 Trolley Square, Salt Lake City, Utah 84102. (natural dyes)

Northwest Handcraft House, 110 West Esplanade, Vancouver, B.C. V7M/1A2, Canada. (natural dyes)

Owl and Olive Weavers, 704 29th St. South, Birmingham, Alabama 35233. (natural dyes)

Paternayan Bros. Inc., 312 E. 95th Street, New York, N.Y. 10028. (yarn)

Village Wools, Fibrecraft Materials and Supplies, 308 San Felipe, N.W., Alburquerque, New Mexico 87104. (natural dyes)

The Yarn Barn, Box 334, 730 Massachusetts, Lawrence, Kansas 66044. (natural dyes)

The Yarnery, 1648 Grand Avenue, St Paul, Minnesota 55105. (natural dyes)

## Scandinavia

Foreningen Hemslöjden, Box 433, Borås, Sweden (Ulla Cyrus loom)

Gunnar Anderssons, Vävskedsverkstad, Oxberg, 729 00 Mora, Sweden (looms)

Vävstolsfabriken Glimakra AB, S-280 64 Glimakra, Sweden (looms)

Anders Lervad and Son, Askov, pr Vejen, Denmark (looms and weaving equipment)

## United Kingdom

Blackstaff Ltd., Springfield Road, Belfast, Northern Ireland (linen)

Craftsman's Mark Ltd., Broadlands, Shortheath, Farnham, Surrey (wool yarns for handweaving and linen for rug warps)

Dryads Handicrafts Ltd., Northgates, Leicester (looms and weaving equipment)

A. K. Graupner, Corner House, Valley Road, Bradford BD1 4AA (2-ply rug wool)

William Hall & Co (Monsall) Ltd., 177 Stanley Road, Cheadle Hulme, Cheadle, Cheshire SK8 6RF (rug wools, cotton yarns)

'Harris' Looms, Northgrove Road, Hawkhurst, Kent TN18 4AP (looms)

Lervad (UK) Ltd., Vernon Building, Westbourne Street, High Wycombe, Bucks (looms)

Hugh MacKay & Co Ltd., P.O. Box 1, Durham City DH1 1SH (rug wools)

Matheson Dyes and Chemicals, Macron Place, London E8 1LP (natural and synthetic dyestuffs)

Multiple Fabric Co Ltd., Dudley Hill, Bradford, BD4 9PD (yarns, horsehair, camel etc)

Russell and Chapple, 23 Monmouth Street, London WC2 (hessian, though this should be generally available through large stores)

Skilbeck Bros. Ltd., 55–57 Glengall Road, London SE15 (synthetic dyestuffs)

# Index

*Page numbers in italics indicate illustrations.*